Classic Steak House Rubbed
Filet Mignon, page 34

# Cooking Light.

# Grilling

Oxmoor House.

ISBN-13: 978-0-8487-3157-1
ISBN-10: 0-8487-3157-3
Library of Congress Control Number:
2006908791
Printed in the United States of America
First printing 2007

Be sure to check with your health-care provider
before making any changes in your diet.

Oxmoor House, Inc.
Editor in Chief: Nancy Fitzpatrick Wyatt
Executive Editor: Katherine M. Eakin
Copy Chief: Allison Long Lowery

*Cooking Light®* Grilling
Editor: Heather Averett
Nutrition Editor: Anne C. Cain, M.P.H.,
    M.S., R.D.
Copy Editor: Jacqueline Giovanelli
Editorial Assistant: Julie Boston
Nutrition Editorial Assistant:
    Rachel Quinlivan, R.D.
Photography Director: Jim Bathie
Senior Photo Stylist: Kay E. Clarke
Photo Stylist: Katherine Eckert
Director, Test Kitchens: Elizabeth Tyler Austin
Assistant Director, Test Kitchens:
    Julie Christopher
Food Stylist: Kelley Self Wilton
Test Kitchens Staff: Kathleen Royal Phillips,
    Catherine Crowell Steele, Ashley T. Strickland
Director of Production: Laura Lockhart
Senior Production Manager: Greg A. Amason
Production Manager: Terri Beste
Production Assistant: Faye Porter Bonner

Contributors:
Designer: Carol Damsky
Indexer: Mary Ann Laurens
Editorial Assistant: Laura K. Womble
Editorial Interns: Jill Baughman, Amy Edgerton,
    Amelia Heying
Photo Stylist: Melanie J. Clarke
Food Stylists: Ana Price Kelly,
    Debby Maugans Nakos
Test Kitchens Staff: Jane Chambliss,
    Kate M. Wheeler, R.D.
Photographer: Beau Gustafson

To order additional publications, call
1-800-765-6400, or visit oxmoorhouse.com

# CONTENTS

## Essential Grilling     8

Basic grilled flank steak, classic
hamburgers, succulent lemon-herb
chicken—here are our best-of-the-best
recipes for grilling. Perfected by *Cooking
Light*, these dishes are so good that only
the cook will know they're light.

## Beef & Lamb     32

Fire up the grill—or grill pan—for
simple steaks, Greek-style burgers, or
spicy beef tenderloin. These sizzling
meats will have you grilling any night
of the week.

## Pork     54

From plum- and prosciutto-stuffed pork
chops to Jamaican jerk pork tenderloin,
you'll find exactly what you need for
mouthwatering suppers.

## Poultry 72

Whether you make a whole beer-can roasted chicken; a citrusy, colorful chicken salad; or a sizzling chicken fajita, you can pull together a meal that's flavor-packed—guaranteed.

## Fish & Shellfish 94

Grilling fish and shellfish makes weeknight meals supereasy. Try something new with sugarcane shrimp skewers, or halibut steak seared to perfection.

## Fruits & Vegetables 116

Fresh, flavorful, and tasty, any of these recipes are a fitting accompaniment to a delicious dinner.

*Cooking Light*®
Editor in Chief: Mary Kay Culpepper
Executive Editor: Billy R. Sims
Art Director: Susan Waldrip Dendy
Managing Editor: Maelynn Cheung
Senior Food Editor: Alison Mann Ashton
Features Editor: Phillip Rhodes
Projects Editor: Mary Simpson Creel, M.S., R.D.
Food Editor: Ann Taylor Pittman
Associate Food Editors: Julianna Grimes Bottcher,
     Timothy Q. Cebula
Assistant Food Editor: Kathy Kitchens Downie, R.D.
Assistant Editors: Cindy Hatcher,
     Brandy Rushing
Test Kitchens Director: Vanessa Taylor Johnson
Senior Food Stylist: Kellie Gerber Kelley
Food Stylist: M. Kathleen Kanen
Test Kitchens Professionals: SaBrina Bone,
     Kathryn Conrad, Mary H. Drennen,
     Jan Jacks Moon, Tiffany Vickers,
     Mike Wilson
Assistant Art Director: Maya Metz Logue
Senior Designers: Fernande Bondarenko,
     J. Shay McNamee
Designer: Brigette Mayer
Senior Photographer: Randy Mayor
Senior Photo Stylist: Cindy Barr
Photo Stylists: Jan Gautro, Leigh Ann Ross
Studio Assistant: Melissa Hoover
Copy Chief: Maria Parker Hopkins
Senior Copy Editor: Susan Roberts
Copy Editor: Johannah Paiva
Production Manager: Liz Rhoades
Production Editors: Joanne McCrary Brasseal,
     Hazel R. Eddins
Administrative Coordinator: Carol D. Johnson
Office Manager: Rita K. Jackson
Editorial Assistant: Abigail Banks
Correspondence Editor: Michelle Gibson Daniels
Intern: Lauri Short

**CookingLight.com**
Editor: Jennifer Middleton Richards
Online Producer: Abigail Masters

Cover: *Adobo Flank Steak with Summer Corn-and-Tomato Relish* (*page 38*)

# Welcome

Grilling is quick, simple, and affords some sizzling prospects for entertaining. But there's another thing that grilling is, and that's essential. For a *Cooking Light®* cook, grilling is a flavorful experience in high-flavor, low-fat cooking.

In this cookbook, you'll find the grilling recipes we believe to be the essential recipes for every *Cooking Light* cook. These recipes are our tried-and-true classics—ones we love to make again and again.

Each chapter offers incredibly simple, fabulously delicious recipes, complete with our trademark nutritional analyses that will help ensure your meals are healthful. After all, eating smart, being fit, and living well are essential in our minds.

So whether you're looking for a down-home recipe for Grilled Chicken with White Barbecue Sauce or for something a little more worldly, such as Argentinean Oak-Planked Beef Tenderloin with Chimichurri Sauce, you're sure to find it in this edition of *The Cooking Light Cook's Essential Recipe Collection*. I hope these recipes will become as essential to your family as they are to the *Cooking Light* family.

Very truly yours,

**Mary Kay Culpepper**
Editor in Chief

# essential grilling

# Basic Grilled Flank Steak

1 (2-pound) flank steak, trimmed
2 teaspoons Worcestershire sauce
½ teaspoon sea salt
½ teaspoon freshly ground black pepper
Cooking spray
Cilantro sprig (optional)

**1.** Place steak in an 11 x 7–inch baking dish. Sprinkle both sides with Worcestershire sauce, salt, and pepper; rub mixture into steak. Cover and refrigerate at least 20 minutes.
**2.** Prepare grill.
**3.** Place steak on a grill rack coated with cooking spray; grill 8 minutes on each side or until desired degree of doneness. Place on a cutting board; cover loosely with foil. Let stand 10 minutes. Cut steak diagonally across grain into thin slices. Garnish with cilantro, if desired. Yield: 8 servings (serving size: 3 ounces).

CALORIES 158 (38% from fat); FAT 6.7g (sat 2.8g, mono 2.7g, poly 0.3g); PROTEIN 22.6g; CARB 0.4g; FIBER 0g; CHOL 45mg; IRON 1.6mg; SODIUM 203mg; CALC 14mg

Flank steak has a distinct, visible grain and should be cut across this grain into ⅛- to ¼-inch-thick slices for maximum tenderness. Tilting your knife diagonally and slicing away from you ensures the largest surface area possible for each piece. Allow 10 minutes of stand time before slicing. During this stand time, the flavorful juices are reabsorbed and redistributed, so they won't run out as freely when you carve.

*An easy marinade gives this steak robust flavor—yet the seasonings are subtle enough that leftovers work in a variety of applications. Try substituting grilled flank steak for the chicken in Sizzling Chicken Fajitas (recipe on page 82) for a hearty dinner, or use it as sandwich meat for tomorrow's lunch.*

# Basic Grilled Steak

4 (6-ounce) ribeye steaks,
   trimmed (about ¾ inch thick)
1 teaspoon salt
¾ teaspoon freshly ground
   black pepper
Cooking spray
Finely chopped fresh parsley
   (optional)

**1.** Sprinkle both sides of steaks with salt and pepper. Let steaks stand at room temperature 20 minutes.
**2.** Prepare grill.
**3.** Pat steaks dry with a paper towel. Place steaks on a grill rack coated with cooking spray; grill 2 minutes on each side or until desired degree of doneness. Remove from grill. Cover steaks loosely with foil; let stand 5 minutes. Garnish with parsley, if desired. Yield: 4 servings (serving size: 1 steak).

CALORIES 275 (46% from fat); FAT 14.1g (sat 5.5g, mono 6.1g, poly 0.5g); PROTEIN 34.3g; CARB 0.3g; FIBER 0.1g; CHOL 100mg; IRON 3.7mg; SODIUM 689mg; CALC 19mg

Tongs, especially those with spring-loaded handles, are the ideal tool for grilling. They can be used with any foods—from thick steaks and hamburgers to thin asparagus spears. Tongs help maintain the shape and juiciness of foods. (A fork will pierce food and cause flavorful juices to escape.) Also, their long slender handles are safer to use than a fork because they keep your hands away from the heat.

*Turn the steaks only once as you cook them. The more time they're in direct contact with the grill, the better. And speaking of better, nothing is better with a grilled steak than sweet, grilled corn-on-the cob. Coat fresh ears of corn with butter-flavored cooking spray; place the corn on the grill rack, and grill over direct heat, covered, 15 to 20 minutes or until the corn is tender, turning occasionally.*

# Classic Hamburgers

1 pound ground round
½ cup quick-cooking oats
¼ cup minced fresh parsley
1 tablespoon Dijon mustard
1 tablespoon Worcestershire
  sauce
½ teaspoon freshly ground
  black pepper
2 garlic cloves, minced
1 small onion, minced (about
  ¾ cup)
1 large egg white
Cooking spray
4 lettuce leaves
4 whole wheat kaiser rolls, split
8 thin slices tomato
4 slices purple onion,
  separated into rings

**1.** Prepare grill.
**2.** Combine first 9 ingredients in a large bowl; stir well. Shape into 4 (¼-inch-thick) patties.
**3.** Place patties on a grill rack coated with cooking spray; cover and grill 5 minutes on each side or until done.
**4.** Place 1 lettuce leaf on bottom half of each roll; place patties on rolls. Top each patty with 2 slices of tomato and 1 slice onion. Yield: 4 servings (serving size: 1 burger).

CALORIES 437 (30% from fat); FAT 14.7g (sat.5.1g, mono 5.8g, poly 1.7g); PROTEIN 31.6g; CARB 43.6g; FIBER 3.5g; CHOL 74mg; IRON 5.6mg; SODIUM 495mg; CALC 100mg

To make sure you're buying lean ground beef, read the label to determine the percentage of fat rather than relying on the name of the specific cut. The percent of lean to fat is usually listed on the label near the name of the cut. For example, "85/15" means that the ground beef is 85% lean and 15% fat. Ground beef with 10% fat or less is sometimes labeled "ground sirloin" or "extra lean." Ground beef with 15% fat is sometimes labeled "ground round." Ground beef with 20% fat is sometimes labeled ground chuck; regular ground beef contains the maximum amount of fat at 30%.

*There's nothing like a good old-fashioned burger hot off the grill, and these are especially mouthwatering. Top these burgers with slices of crisp, green lettuce, juicy red-ripe tomatoes, zingy purple onion, and a whole wheat kaiser roll. It's a burger as classic as they come.*

# Rosemary Grilled Lamb Chops

1 tablespoon chopped fresh
  rosemary
1 teaspoon olive oil
½ teaspoon kosher salt,
  divided
1 garlic clove, minced
4 (4-ounce) lamb loin chops,
  trimmed
⅛ teaspoon freshly ground
  black pepper
Cooking spray
Rosemary sprigs (optional)

**1.** Combine rosemary, oil, ¼ teaspoon salt, and garlic; rub mixture evenly over both sides of lamb. Cover and marinate in refrigerator at least 2 hours or overnight.
**2.** Prepare grill.
**3.** Remove lamb from bag. Sprinkle both sides of lamb with ¼ teaspoon salt and pepper. Place lamb on a grill rack coated with cooking spray; grill 3 minutes on each side or until desired degree of doneness (145° for medium-rare). Garnish with rosemary sprigs, if desired. Yield: 4 servings (serving size: 1 chop).

CALORIES 278 (54% from fat); FAT 16.8g (sat 7.5g, mono 7.1g, poly 0.8g); PROTEIN 29.3g; CARB 0.4g; FIBER 0.1g; CHOL 96mg; IRON 2.7mg; SODIUM 308mg; CALC 19mg

Overcooked lamb can be tough and flavorless, so use an instant-read thermometer to determine when to remove the lamb from the grill (from 145° for medium-rare to 170° for well done). Insert the instant-read thermometer into the lamb near the end of the recommended cooking time. After the temperature of the meat registers, remove the thermometer.

*Garlic and chopped fresh rosemary lend a heady fragrant aroma to a humble lamb chop. Marinating the lamb chops in olive oil along with your seasonings of choice allows the meat to soak up a variety of rich flavors, yet doesn't overpower the essence of the lamb.*

# Hickory-Planked Pork Tenderloin with Rosemary-Dijon Potatoes

1 (15 x 6½ x ⅜-inch) hickory grilling plank
¼ cup Dijon mustard
1 tablespoon honey
½ teaspoon freshly ground black pepper
½ teaspoon chopped fresh rosemary
2 garlic cloves, minced
1 (1-pound) pork tenderloin, trimmed
2 cups (¼-inch-thick) slices red potato (about 8 ounces)
1 tablespoon fresh lemon juice
Rosemary sprig (optional)

**1.** Immerse and soak plank in water 1 hour; drain.
**2.** To prepare grill for indirect grilling, heat one side of grill to high heat.
**3.** Combine mustard, honey, pepper, rosemary, and garlic, stirring well with a whisk. Brush half of mustard mixture over pork.
**4.** Place potato in a microwave-safe bowl, and cover with plastic wrap. Microwave at HIGH 1 minute. Add remaining mustard mixture and juice; toss gently to coat.
**5.** Place plank on grill rack over high heat; grill 5 minutes or until lightly charred. Carefully turn plank over; move to cool side of grill. Place pork in middle of charred side of plank; arrange potato mixture around pork in a single layer. Cover and grill 50 minutes or until a meat thermometer registers 160° (slightly pink). Garnish with rosemary, if desired. Yield: 4 servings (serving size: 3 ounces pork and ⅓ cup potatoes).

CALORIES 216 (22% from fat); FAT 5.3g (sat 1.4g, mono 2.2g, poly 0.8g); PROTEIN 26g; CARB 16.1g; FIBER 1.3g; CHOL 74mg; IRON 2.3mg; SODIUM 439mg; CALC 37mg

A smoldering hickory plank lends a subtly smoky note that complements the flavors of the pork and potatoes in this recipe without overwhelming them. Wood planks suited for grilling are widely available, conveniently packaged, and sized to fit standard grills. They're available seasonally from barbecue and gourmet stores (like Williams-Sonoma); seafood markets often stock them year-round. You can also order planks online from www.barbecuewood.com. Planks vary from about $3 to $4 apiece in stores (they usually come in packs of 3 or 4) to $8 to $9 apiece (including shipping) on the Internet.

*The mustard glaze does double duty on the pork and potatoes. Jump-start the potatoes in the microwave before putting them on the grill so they'll be done at the same time as the pork. The taste and aroma of the potatoes, pork, rosemary, and hickory blend together for an unforgettable meal.*

# Grilled Lemon-Herb Chicken

In this recipe, the chicken is first split and then butterflied (flattened), a technique that allows for quicker and more uniform cooking. Rather than cutting through the breastbone, flip the chicken over and use kitchen shears to cut down the backbone. Once the chicken is cut, it will open up and lie flat on the grill for even cooking.

1 (5-pound) roasting chicken
3 tablespoons fresh lemon
  juice
2 tablespoons chopped fresh
  parsley
1 tablespoon chopped fresh
  thyme
1 teaspoon salt
½ teaspoon freshly ground
  black pepper
Cooking spray
Lemon wedges (optional)
Parsley sprigs (optional)
Thyme sprigs (optional)

**1.** Remove and discard giblets and neck from chicken. Rinse chicken with cold water, and pat dry. Trim excess fat. Place chicken, breast side down, on a cutting surface. Cut chicken in half lengthwise along backbone (do not cut through breastbone). Turn chicken over. Starting at neck cavity, loosen skin from breast and drumsticks by inserting fingers, gently pushing between skin and meat.

**2.** Combine juice and next 4 ingredients; rub mixture under loosened skin and over breast and drumsticks. Gently press skin to secure. Place chicken in a large zip-top plastic bag. Seal and marinate in refrigerator 30 minutes.

**3.** Prepare grill.

**4.** Place chicken, skin side up, on a grill rack coated with cooking spray. Grill 55 minutes or until a thermometer inserted into meaty part of thigh registers 180°. Remove chicken from grill; cover and let stand 10 minutes. Remove and discard skin. Garnish with lemon wedges, parsley sprigs, and thyme sprigs, if desired. Yield: 5 servings (serving size: about 4 ounces).

CALORIES 203 (27% from fat); FAT 6.2g (sat 1.7g, mono 2.2g, poly 1.4g); PROTEIN 33.5g; CARB 1.1g; FIBER 0.2g; CHOL 100mg; IRON 1.5mg; SODIUM 565mg; CALC 21mg

*If your grill is large enough, cook two chickens at the same time to feed a larger group or just to have more leftovers for quick lunches. Or, if you don't want to use a whole bird, use chicken pieces, and grill for a shorter amount of time. Refrigerate any leftover chicken up to three days.*

# Grilled Chicken with White Barbecue Sauce

Leaving the skin on the chicken preserves its natural moisture during grilling. To season the breast halves, loosen the skin by inserting your fingers and gently rubbing the seasonings under the skin.

**Chicken:**
- 8 (8-ounce) bone-in chicken breast halves
- 1 teaspoon salt
- 1 teaspoon onion powder
- 1 teaspoon garlic powder
- 1 teaspoon paprika
- 1 teaspoon chipotle chile powder
- Cooking spray

**Sauce:**
- ½ cup light mayonnaise
- ⅓ cup white vinegar
- 1 tablespoon coarsely ground black pepper
- ½ teaspoon ground red pepper
- 1½ teaspoons fresh lemon juice
- Dash of salt

**1.** Prepare grill, heating to medium-hot using both burners.

**2.** To prepare chicken, loosen skin from breasts by inserting fingers, gently pushing between skin and meat. Combine salt and next 4 ingredients, and rub under loosened skin.

**3.** Turn left burner off (leave right burner on). Coat grill rack with cooking spray. Place chicken on grill rack over right burner; grill 5 minutes on each side or until browned. Move chicken to grill rack over left burner. Cover and cook 35 minutes or until done, turning once. Remove chicken from grill.

**4.** To prepare sauce, combine mayonnaise and remaining 5 ingredients, stirring with a whisk. Serve with chicken. Yield: 8 servings (serving size: 1 breast half and about 2 tablespoons sauce).

CALORIES 252 (25% from fat); FAT 6.9g (sat 1.3g, mono 1.4g, poly 3.4g); PROTEIN 34.4g; CARB 10.9g; FIBER 0.6g; CHOL 91mg; IRON 1.5mg; SODIUM 536mg; CALC 26mg

*White barbecue sauce—featuring mayonnaise, vinegar, lemon juice, and pepper—is a tangy alternative to a sweet and spicy barbecue sauce. If serving it for a weeknight dinner to finicky eaters, you may want to cut back on the spices you put on the chicken, as they do generate quite a kick.*

# Orange-and-Bourbon Grilled Salmon

The natural oils in fresh salmon make it an excellent fish for grilling. For best results, keep the salmon skin intact while grilling. The skin prevents salmon from curling up and flaking apart. Grill salmon until the meat begins to change color and becomes flaky. If salmon is overcooked, it becomes dry and loses flavor. When grilled right, salmon will fall apart at the prick of your fork and melt in your mouth.

¼ cup bourbon
¼ cup fresh orange juice
¼ cup low-sodium soy sauce
¼ cup packed brown sugar
¼ cup chopped green onions
3 tablespoons chopped fresh chives
2 tablespoons fresh lemon juice
2 garlic cloves, chopped
4 (6-ounce) salmon fillets (about 1 inch thick)
Cooking spray
Lemon wedges (optional)
Green onion strips (optional)

**1.** Combine first 8 ingredients in a large zip-top plastic bag, and add salmon to bag. Seal and marinate in refrigerator 1½ hours, turning bag occasionally.
**2.** Prepare grill.
**3.** Remove salmon from bag, reserving marinade. Place salmon on a grill rack coated with cooking spray. Cook 6 minutes on each side or until fish flakes easily when tested with a fork, basting frequently with reserved marinade. Garnish with lemon wedges and green onion strips, if desired. Yield: 4 servings (serving size: 1 fillet).

CALORIES 365 (35% from fat); FAT 14.1g (sat 2.5g, mono 6.8g, poly 3.1g); PROTEIN 36g; CARB 18g; FIBER 0.3g; CHOL 111mg; IRON 1.4mg; SODIUM 575mg; CALC 34mg

*To make a complete meal, serve the salmon over a bed of brown rice, with green beans and a salad on the side. Save some orange-and-bourbon marinade and drizzle over the salmon and rice to impart complementing flavors of bourbon and citrus throughout.*

# Grilled Lemon-Bay Shrimp

2 tablespoons fresh lemon
   juice
1 tablespoon olive oil
½ teaspoon salt
½ teaspoon crushed red pepper
½ teaspoon freshly ground
   black pepper
2 garlic cloves, minced
32 large shrimp
32 fresh bay leaves
4 large lemons, each cut into
   8 wedges
Cooking spray

1. Prepare grill.
2. Peel shrimp, leaving tails intact.
3. Combine first 6 ingredients in a large bowl. Add shrimp; toss to coat. Cover and marinate in refrigerator 10 minutes.
4. Place bay leaves and lemon wedges in a large bowl. Coat with cooking spray; toss to coat.
5. Thread 4 lemon wedges, 4 shrimp, and 4 bay leaves alternately onto each of 8 (10-inch) skewers. Place skewers on a grill rack coated with cooking spray, and grill 2 minutes on each side or until shrimp are done. Yield: 4 servings (serving size: 2 kebabs).

CALORIES 217 (27% from fat); FAT 6.4g (sat 1g, mono 2.9g, poly 1.4g); PROTEIN 34.8g; CARB 3.1g; FIBER 0.3g; CHOL 259mg; IRON 4.3mg; SODIUM 545mg; CALC 94mg

For easy grilling, choose large or jumbo shrimp and thread them onto metal or wooden skewers. There is a wide variety of shrimp that come in slightly different colors. Most fresh, uncooked shrimp start out a grayish color, almost blue, and turn pink as they cook. Shrimp is done once the skin surface of the shrimp no longer shows any of its original color. Quickly remove shrimp from the heat as soon as they're done. Overcooked shrimp has a rubbery texture and is tasteless.

*The simplicity of this dish belies its incredible taste. Bay leaves and lemon wedges infuse peppered shrimp with woodsy and citrus flavors. If your grocery store doesn't carry fresh bay leaves, substitute good-quality dried bay leaves (such as Spice Island) soaked overnight in water. Leave the tails on the shrimp for a prettier presentation.*

# Grilled Mexican Corn with Crema

1 teaspoon chipotle chile powder
½ teaspoon salt
⅛ teaspoon freshly ground black pepper
6 ears fresh corn
Cooking spray
¼ cup crema Mexicana or low-fat sour cream
6 lime wedges (optional)

**1.** Prepare grill.

**2.** Combine first 3 ingredients.

**3.** Place corn on a grill rack coated with cooking spray; cook 12 minutes or until corn is lightly browned, turning frequently. Place corn on a platter; drizzle with crema. Sprinkle with chile powder mixture. Garnish with lime wedges, if desired. Yield: 6 servings (serving size: 1 ear).

CALORIES 160 (29% from fat); FAT 5.2g (sat 2.5g, mono 1.5g, poly 1g); PROTEIN 5g; CARB 28.2g; FIBER 4g; CHOL 8mg; IRON 0.8mg; SODIUM 228mg; CALC 24mg

We've experimented a lot to find the best and easiest ways to get a grilled taste without overcooking the corn. We don't like to soak the husks first in cold water as many do because that steams the corn on the grill. We prefer to either grill the corn in the husks without soaking so that the husks char a bit on the outside and transmit some of that flavor to the kernels, or to husk it and grill the nude ears directly over the heat.

*On the streets of Mexico, people line up at vendor carts to buy giant ears of roasted corn dunked in rich crema Mexicana and sprinkled with chili powder and lime juice. This savory treat provides a festive twist to the basic corn-on-the-cob. Crema Mexicana is a sweet, heavy cream that ranges in flavor from tangy to mildly bland with a slightly stiff to thick consistency. If you have difficulty finding it, use low-fat sour cream as a substitute.*

# Grilled Stone Fruit Antipasto Plate

Fruit is perfect for grilling because it's so simple to prepare. With most fruits, all you have to do is cut them in half and place them on the grill. Firm fruits hold up best while softer fruits, like peaches and plums, require a little more attention. If overcooked, soft fruits can become mushy. Choose a fresh, firm fruit that is almost perfectly ripe. For this particular recipe we've chosen stone fruits including plums, peaches, nectarines, and pluots.

**Dressing:**
  3 tablespoons white balsamic vinegar
  2 tablespoons extravirgin olive oil
  2 tablespoons fresh lime juice
  1 tablespoon brown sugar
  2 teaspoons vanilla extract
  ¼ teaspoon freshly ground black pepper
  ⅛ teaspoon salt
  ⅛ teaspoon hot sauce

**Fruit:**
  1 pound firm black plums, halved and pitted
  1 pound firm peaches, halved and pitted
  ½ pound firm nectarines, halved and pitted
  ½ pound firm pluots, halved and pitted
Cooking spray
Chopped fresh mint (optional)

1. Prepare grill.
2. To prepare dressing, combine first 8 ingredients in a small bowl, stirring well with a whisk.
3. To prepare fruit, place fruit on a grill rack coated with cooking spray; grill 3 minutes on each side. Remove from grill. Drizzle fruit with dressing. Garnish with mint, if desired. Yield: 8 servings.

CALORIES 129 (29% from fat); FAT 4.1g (sat 0.5g, mono 2.9g, poly 0.4g); PROTEIN 1.4g; CARB 23.8g; FIBER 2.9g; CHOL 0mg; IRON 0.3mg; SODIUM 39mg; CALC 12mg

*Black pepper and vanilla heighten the sweetness of the stone fruit. Make sure to clean the cooking grate thoroughly so that no residue from previously grilled foods ruins the flavor of the fruit.*

# beef & lamb

# Classic Steak House Rubbed Filet Mignon

2 teaspoons black peppercorns
¼ teaspoon dried rosemary
1 teaspoon dry mustard
¾ teaspoon kosher salt
½ teaspoon garlic powder
4 (4-ounce) beef tenderloin
    steaks, trimmed (1 inch thick)
Cooking spray

**1.** Prepare grill.
**2.** Place peppercorns and rosemary in a spice or coffee grinder; pulse until pepper is coarsely ground.
**3.** Combine pepper mixture, dry mustard, salt, and garlic powder; rub evenly over both sides of steaks. Place steaks on a grill rack coated with cooking spray, and grill 3 minutes on each side or until desired degree of doneness. Yield: 4 servings (serving size: 1 steak).

CALORIES 188 (43% from fat); FAT 8.9g (sat 3.2g, mono 3.3g, poly 0.3g); PROTEIN 24.5g; CARB 0.8g; FIBER 0.2g; CHOL 72mg; IRON 3.3mg; SODIUM 407mg; CALC 11mg

For an attractive presentation, grill crosshatches on the steak. First, place the steak on the grill. After about a minute—or halfway through the cooking time for the first side of the steak—rotate the meat a quarter-turn (45° for diamond-shaped crosshatches, 90° for square-shaped marks). Next, flip the steak over, and complete cooking. Don't flip steak back onto the marked side while grilling. Only one side of the steak will show on the plate, so both sides don't need crosshatches.

*Filet mignon and beef tenderloin steaks are the same cut of meat. For the leanest, juiciest, and most flavorful steaks, look for those that are richly marbled, but well-trimmed of exterior fat. The rub, which includes pungent dry mustard powder, fiery crushed black peppercorns, and fragrant rosemary, makes this choice cut of beef even better.*

# Argentinean Oak-Planked Beef Tenderloin with Chimichurri Sauce

Unlike plain grilled meats, which can dry out and become tough and flavorless when left over the flames too long, meat cooked on a well-soaked plank remains moist and tender. Additionally, the meat absorbs flavor from the smoldering plank, subtle to robust, depending on the type of wood used for the plank. An oak plank provides a medium aroma. Expect an acidic note without any bitterness (similar to the flavor oak imparts to chardonnay). For more information on planks, see page 18.

**Steaks:**

1 (15 x 6 ½ x ⅜–inch) oak grilling plank
4 (4-ounce) beef tenderloin steaks, trimmed (¾ inch thick)
½ teaspoon salt
¼ teaspoon freshly ground black pepper

**Sauce:**

¾ cup fresh flat-leaf parsley leaves
¼ cup fresh cilantro leaves
¼ cup fresh mint leaves
¼ cup chopped onion
¼ cup fat-free, less-sodium chicken broth
3 tablespoons sherry vinegar
2 tablespoons fresh oregano leaves
1 teaspoon olive oil
½ teaspoon salt
½ teaspoon freshly ground black pepper
½ teaspoon crushed red pepper
3 garlic cloves

**1.** Immerse and soak plank in water 1 hour; drain.
**2.** Prepare grill, heating one side to medium and one side to high heat.
**3.** To prepare steaks, sprinkle steaks with ½ teaspoon salt and ¼ teaspoon black pepper. Place plank on a grill rack over high heat; grill 5 minutes or until lightly charred. Carefully turn plank over; move to medium heat. Place steak on charred side of plank. Cover and grill 12 minutes or until desired degree of doneness.
**4.** To prepare sauce, place parsley and remaining 11 ingredients in a food processor; process until smooth. Serve with steaks. Yield: 4 servings (serving size: 1 steak and 1½ tablespoons sauce).

CALORIES 159 (31% from fat); FAT 5.5g (sat 1.7g, mono 2.4g, poly 0.1g); PROTEIN 23.3g; CARB 5.7g; FIBER 1.4g; CHOL 60mg; IRON 4.4mg; SODIUM 977mg; CALC 52mg

*Grilled steak topped with emerald-colored chimichurri is one of Argentina's national dishes. Considered the barbecue sauce of Argentina, chimichurri is built on garlic and parsley, and is also a pungent cross between vinaigrette and pesto. Mint gives this version a more delicate taste.*

# Adobo Flank Steak with Summer Corn-and-Tomato Relish

To season the grill to prevent food from sticking and to help keep the grill clean, lightly coat the grate with cooking spray or with an oil that has a high smoke point (such as peanut oil) before turning on the grill. Be sure not to spray or spread oil on the grate when the grill is hot.

**Steak:**
- 1 teaspoon black peppercorns
- 1 teaspoon cumin seeds
- 2 whole cloves
- 1 (7-ounce) can chipotle chiles in adobo sauce, undrained
- 2 tablespoons sherry vinegar
- 1 tablespoon fresh thyme leaves
- 2 teaspoons brown sugar
- ¾ teaspoon kosher salt
- 1 garlic clove, peeled
- 1 (1¼-pound) flank steak, trimmed
- Cooking spray

**Relish:**
- 2 cups fresh corn kernels (about 4 ears)
- 1 cup chopped seeded tomato
- ¼ cup chopped bottled roasted red bell peppers
- 2 tablespoons sherry vinegar
- 1 tablespoon extravirgin olive oil
- ¾ teaspoon kosher salt
- Fresh thyme leaves (optional)

1. To prepare steak, cook first 3 ingredients in a small non-stick skillet over medium heat 45 seconds or until toasted. Place peppercorn mixture in a spice or coffee grinder; process until finely ground.

2. Remove 1 chile from can; reserve remaining chiles and sauce for another use. Place peppercorn mixture, chile, 2 tablespoons vinegar, and next 4 ingredients in a blender; process until smooth, scraping sides occasionally. Combine vinegar mixture and steak in a large zip-top plastic bag; seal and marinate in refrigerator 24 hours. Remove from bag; discard marinade.

3. Prepare grill.

4. Place steak on a grill rack coated with cooking spray, and cook 6 minutes on each side or until desired degree of doneness. Cut steak diagonally across grain into thin slices.

5. To prepare relish, heat a large nonstick skillet over medium-high heat; coat pan with cooking spray. Add corn; sauté 5 minutes or until lightly browned. Remove from heat; stir in tomato and next 4 ingredients. Serve with steak. Garnish with thyme, if desired. Yield: 5 servings (serving size: 3 ounces steak and ½ cup relish).

CALORIES 303 (44% from fat); FAT 14.9g (sat 5.2g, mono 6.7g, poly 1.3g); PROTEIN 25.2g; CARB 16.5g; FIBER 2.7g; CHOL 57mg; IRON 3.2mg; SODIUM 634mg; CALC 20mg

*Sherry vinegar, with its sour-sweet flavor and deep notes of oak, is the secret ingredient in the relish. The vinegar marries and extends the flavors of the roasted corn and peppers and acidic tomatoes creating a relish that tames the spicy heat of the flank steak. Sherry vinegar is also delicious on grilled vegetable salads, especially those featuring zucchini, bell peppers, and chiles.*

*(pictured on cover)*

# Grilled Porterhouse Steak

1 (2-pound) porterhouse steak (about 1½ inches thick)
2 tablespoons Worcestershire sauce
1 teaspoon sea or kosher salt
1 teaspoon coarsely ground black pepper
Cooking spray
1 teaspoon unsalted butter, softened

**1.** Place steak in a dish. Coat steak with Worcestershire sauce. Cover; marinate in refrigerator 30 minutes, turning occasionally.

**2.** Prepare grill, heating one side to medium and one side to high heat.

**3.** Remove steak from Worcestershire sauce; discard sauce. Sprinkle steak with 1 teaspoon salt and 1 teaspoon pepper; let stand at room temperature 15 minutes. Place steak on a grill rack coated with cooking spray over high heat; grill 3 minutes on each side. Turn steak, and place over medium heat; grill 3 minutes on each side or until desired degree of doneness. Place steak on a platter. Rub butter over top of steak; let stand 10 minutes. Yield: 6 servings (serving size: 3 ounces).

CALORIES 205 (32% from fat); FAT 7.3g (sat 2.7g, mono 2.8g, poly 0.3g); PROTEIN 33.2g; CARB 0.8g; FIBER 3.1g; CHOL 94mg; IRON 4.2mg; SODIUM 499mg; CALC 15mg

Look for a porterhouse steak that's approximately 1- to 1½-inches-thick. Keep the smaller, more tender tip of the steak angled away from the hottest part of the fire to prevent it from cooking too quickly. Generally, we recommend only turning the steak once, but for the best flavor and tenderness we grilled the steak first over high heat and finished grilling over medium heat, turning both times. To test for doneness, cut into the steak with the tip of a knife and peek, or insert an instant-read thermometer into the side of the steak—medium-rare will register 145°.

*Steak and cabernet sauvignon make a classic American combo. The char and meatiness of the steak are beautifully offset by the structure of the wine. If you have a large enough grill, start grilling Grilled Fries, recipe on page 124, with the steak so everything will be done at the same time. Otherwise, tent the beef with foil to keep it warm.*

# Hoisin Grilled Sirloin

2 tablespoons hoisin sauce
1 tablespoon apricot preserves
1½ teaspoons fresh lime juice
⅛ teaspoon crushed red
    pepper
½ teaspoon salt
1 pound top sirloin

1. Heat a grill pan over medium-high heat.
2. Combine first 4 ingredients, stirring with a whisk.
3. Sprinkle salt over beef. Add beef to pan; cook 3 minutes on each side or until desired degree of doneness. Let stand 5 minutes before slicing. Brush both sides of beef with hoisin mixture. Cut beef across grain into thin slices. Yield: 4 servings (serving size: about 3 ounces).

CALORIES 213 (37% from fat); FAT 8.8g (sat 3.4g, mono 3.7g, poly 0.5g); PROTEIN 25.3g; CARB 7g; FIBER 0.3g; CHOL 76mg; IRON 2.9mg; SODIUM 477mg; CALC 13mg

A grill pan is a good alternative to a gas or charcoal grill. With ridges that elevate food so air can circulate underneath and fat can drip away, a grill pan adds more than just pretty grill marks and smoky flavors. Your food doesn't sauté or steam as it does in a plain skillet; instead, flavor is seared into the food. Meat and fish turn out juicy, with no need for added fat. Vegetables stay crisp-tender, and their nutrients don't leach out.

*Hoisin sauce is thick, sweet, and spicy. It's most commonly used as a dipping sauce for a variety of Chinese dishes. Brushing the grilled sirloin with the hoisin mixture gives your meat added flavor. You can find hoisin sauce in Asian markets and large supermarkets. Serve the sirloin with snow peas and rice for a balanced meal.*

# Grilled Sirloin Kebabs with Peaches and Peppers

To ensure even cooking when grilling kebabs, make sure the pieces of food are all the same size. For the peaches, onions, and peppers in this recipe, try to cut them in roughly the same size. If you want to grill chicken instead of beef for these kebabs, pound the chicken to an even thickness so it cooks quickly and evenly.

**Kebabs:**
1½ tablespoons ground cumin
1½ tablespoons cracked black pepper
2¾ teaspoons kosher salt
2 pounds boneless sirloin steak, cut into 48 (1-inch) pieces
4 peaches, each cut into 8 wedges
2 small red onions, each cut into 8 wedges
2 large red bell peppers, each cut into 8 (1-inch) pieces
Cooking spray
**Sauce:**
½ cup chopped fresh parsley
¼ cup red wine vinegar
1 teaspoon olive oil
¼ teaspoon kosher salt
¼ teaspoon cracked black pepper
3 garlic cloves, minced
Parsley sprigs (optional)

**1.** Prepare grill.
**2.** To prepare kebabs, combine first 7 ingredients; toss well. Thread 3 steak pieces, 2 peach wedges, 1 onion wedge, and 1 bell pepper piece alternately onto each of 16 (12-inch) skewers. Place skewers on a grill rack coated with cooking spray; grill 6 minutes or until tender, turning occasionally. Place on a platter; cover loosely with foil. Let stand 5 minutes.
**3.** To prepare sauce, combine chopped parsley and next 5 ingredients, stirring with a whisk. Spoon over kebabs. Garnish with parsley sprigs, if desired. Yield: 8 servings (serving size: 2 kebabs).
**Note:** If using wooden skewers, soak them in water 30 minutes before grilling.

CALORIES 217 (30% from fat); FAT 7.2g (sat 2.4g, mono 3g, poly 0.4g); PROTEIN 25.5g; CARB 12.4g; FIBER 3.2g; CHOL 69mg; IRON 3.8mg; SODIUM 768mg; CALC 38mg

*Kebabs are great for entertaining because they're as easy to serve as they are to prepare. If you're expecting vegetarians, cook the meat and vegetables on separate skewers, so guests who don't want meat can pick up a kebab of vegetables. If your guests assemble their own skewers, place the meat and vegetables in separate bowls.*

# Greek-Style Burgers with Feta Aïoli

Feta cheese, often referred to as pickled cheese, is a classic Greek cheese that's stored and cured in its own whey brine. Aïoli is a strongly flavored garlic mayonnaise. Mixing these distinct cultural favorites together creates an unforgettable spread for your burgers.

**Aïoli:**
- ½ cup (2 ounces) crumbled feta cheese
- 2 tablespoons light mayonnaise
- 2 tablespoons plain fat-free yogurt
- ¼ teaspoon coarsely ground black pepper
- 1 garlic clove, minced

**Burgers:**
- 5 (½-inch-thick) slices red onion
- Cooking spray
- 1 pound ground round
- ⅔ cup breadcrumbs
- ⅓ cup chopped bottled roasted red bell peppers
- ¼ cup chopped fresh parsley
- 1 teaspoon dried oregano
- ¼ teaspoon salt
- ¼ teaspoon coarsely ground black pepper
- 1 (10-ounce) package frozen chopped spinach, thawed, drained, and squeezed dry
- 1 large egg, lightly beaten
- 2 garlic cloves, crushed
- 5 (1½-ounce) sourdough sandwich buns

**1.** To prepare aïoli, place first 5 ingredients in a food processor; pulse 1 minute or until smooth. Cover and chill.
**2.** Prepare grill.
**3.** To prepare burgers, place onion slices on a grill rack coated with cooking spray, and cook 2 minutes on each side. Set aside.
**4.** Combine beef and next 9 ingredients in a large bowl. Divide beef mixture into 5 equal portions, shaping each portion into a ½-inch-thick patty. Place patties on grill rack coated with cooking spray, and cook 6 minutes on each side or until burgers are done. Spread 1½ tablespoons aïoli evenly over top and bottom half of each bun. Place patties on bottom halves of buns, and top each with onion and top half of bun. Yield: 5 servings (serving size: 1 burger).

CALORIES 385 (28% from fat); FAT 12.1g (sat 4.4g, mono 4.4g, poly 1.8g); PROTEIN 30.5g; CARB 38g; FIBER 4.3g; CHOL 110mg; IRON 5.7mg; SODIUM 712mg; CALC 225mg

*This burger—stuffed with roasted bell peppers and spinach—carries Greek flavors in every bite. Greek cuisine highlights healthy ingredients such as fresh vegetables and olive oil, so these burgers are a filling, lighter alternative to traditional hamburgers.*

# Blue Cheese-Stuffed Burgers

Cooking spray
½ cup finely chopped onion
1 pound ground round
3 tablespoons dry breadcrumbs
2 tablespoons water
1 egg white, lightly beaten
¼ cup (1 ounce) crumbled blue cheese
¼ cup fat-free sour cream
4 (1-ounce) English muffins, toasted
4 lettuce leaves
4 (¼-inch-thick) slices tomato

**1.** Heat a small nonstick skillet over medium heat; coat pan with cooking spray. Add onion; sauté 5 minutes or until tender. Remove from heat; let cool.
**2.** Combine onion, beef, breadcrumbs, water, and egg white in a large bowl; stir well. Divide mixture into 8 equal portions, shaping each into a ½-inch-thick patty. Spoon 1 tablespoon cheese into center of 4 patties; top with remaining patties. Press edges together to seal.
**3.** Prepare grill.
**4.** Place patties on a grill rack coated with cooking spray; grill 4 minutes on each side or until done.
**5.** Spread 1 tablespoon sour cream over top half of each muffin, and set aside. Line bottom halves of muffins with lettuce leaves; top each with a tomato slice, a patty, and top half of muffin. Yield: 4 servings (serving size: 1 burger).

CALORIES 327 (28% from fat); FAT 10.3g (sat 3.9g, mono 3.7g, poly 0.7g); PROTEIN 31.4g; CARB 25.1g; FIBER 1g; CHOL 75mg; IRON 3.8mg; SODIUM 391mg; CALC 116mg

Stuffing burgers is easy. Divide the beef mixture into 8 equal portions; shape each portion into a ½-inch-thick patty. Spoon the cheese or other ingredient of choice into the center of 4 patties, and top with the remaining patties. Press or pinch the edges together to seal. Make sure the edges are sealed tightly so the cheese doesn't leak out during the cooking process. Stuffing burgers ensures an equal amount of cheesy flavor in every bite.

*A traditional hamburger patty gets a makeover when you add onion, breadcrumbs, and egg white to the meat. Using English muffins, which are usually smaller than buns, allows the blue cheese and the meat to dominate the flavors in this recipe. Try stuffing these burgers with shredded Cheddar or Swiss cheese if you don't like blue cheese.*

# Grilled Lamb Chops

3 tablespoons dried oregano
1 teaspoon salt
½ teaspoon freshly ground
   black pepper
8 (4-ounce) lamb loin chops,
   trimmed
4 garlic cloves, thinly sliced
3 tablespoons dry sherry
Cooking spray
Lime wedges (optional)

**1.** Combine first 3 ingredients; sprinkle evenly over lamb. Place lamb in a heavy-duty zip-top plastic bag. Add garlic and sherry; seal bag, turning to coat. Marinate in refrigerator 3 hours, turning occasionally.
**2.** Prepare grill.
**3.** Place lamb on a grill rack coated with cooking spray; cook 5 minutes on each side or until desired degree of doneness. Serve with lime wedges, if desired. Yield: 4 servings (serving size: 2 chops).

CALORIES 273 (31% from fat); FAT 9.4g (sat 3.7g, mono 3.8g, poly 0.5g); PROTEIN 39.1g; CARB 3.4g; FIBER 1.5g; CHOL 120mg; IRON 5.6mg; SODIUM 705mg; CALC 76mg

You can use two traditional methods to perk up the flavors of meat, poultry, or seafood before you grill—one wet, one dry. This recipe combines both methods, a dry rub and a wet marinade. A heavy-duty zip-top plastic bag is ideal since you can turn the bag rather than each piece of food. Generally speaking, the longer you marinate a food, the stronger it will taste. Always marinate in the refrigerator.

*Lamb pairs well with the bold flavors of many ethnic cuisines, but you'll find it tasty and suitable with simple seasonings, too. Use dry white wine instead of sherry, if you like.*

# Yogurt-Marinated Lamb Kebabs

Skewering small chunks of meat and vegetables on wooden sticks or long, thin pointed metal rods is a grilling tradition. Soak wooden skewers in water for at least 30 minutes before using them or they'll burn. Wooden skewers should be discarded after use. If you grill often, invest in a set of metal skewers, which can be reused and require no soaking.

½ pound lean boneless leg of lamb
¼ cup plain fat-free yogurt
1 tablespoon finely chopped onion
2 teaspoons olive oil
1½ teaspoons ground cumin
½ teaspoon dried rosemary
½ teaspoon pepper
¼ teaspoon salt
1 garlic clove, minced
2 cups (1-inch) sliced zucchini
6 large cherry tomatoes
1 small onion, cut into 4 wedges
Cooking spray
2 cups cooked couscous

**1.** Trim fat from lamb. Cut lamb into 1-inch pieces.
**2.** Combine yogurt and next 7 ingredients in a large zip-top plastic bag. Add lamb; seal bag, and marinate in refrigerator 8 hours, turning bag occasionally. Remove lamb from bag, reserving marinade.
**3.** Thread lamb, zucchini, tomatoes, and onion wedges alternately onto 4 (10-inch) skewers.
**4.** Prepare grill.
**5.** Place kebabs on a grill rack coated with cooking spray; grill 7 minutes on each side or until done, basting occasionally with reserved marinade. Serve kebabs with couscous. Yield: 2 servings (serving size: 2 kebabs and 1 cup couscous).
**Note:** If using wooden skewers, soak them in water 30 minutes before grilling.

CALORIES 464 (25% from fat); FAT 12.8g (sat 3.1g, mono 6.5g, poly 1g); PROTEIN 35.4g; CARB 53.1g; FIBER 4.3g; CHOL 76mg; IRON 5mg; SODIUM 390mg; CALC 116mg

*Kebabs create a mouthwatering variation to the routine appearance of your dinner plate, and they're more time-friendly. Because they cook so fast, you'll be able to enjoy your guests instead of standing over a hot grill.*

# pork

# Adobo-Marinated Pork Tenderloin with Grilled-Pineapple Salsa

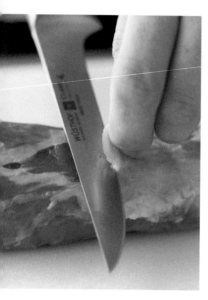

When preparing the tenderloin, remove the silver skin, which is the thin, shiny membrane that runs along the surface of the meat. Leaving the silver skin on can cause the tenderloin to toughen and lose shape during grilling. Stretching the membrane with one hand so it's tight, use your other hand to slip the tip of the knife underneath the silvery skin. Slowly slice back and forth, angling the sharp edge of the blade up, rather than down, through the meat. Continue this process until all the silver skin is removed, then discard.

1 cup fresh lime juice
2 teaspoons black pepper
2 teaspoons dried oregano
2 teaspoons ground cumin
1½ teaspoons salt
6 garlic cloves, crushed
2 pounds pork tenderloin
1½ teaspoons olive oil
Cooking spray
¼ cup coarsely chopped fresh cilantro
2 tablespoons finely chopped green onions
Grilled-Pineapple Salsa

**1.** Combine first 6 ingredients in a 2-quart baking dish. Trim fat from pork. Place pork in dish, turning to coat; cover and marinate in refrigerator 1 hour, turning pork occasionally.
**2.** Prepare grill.
**3.** Remove pork from dish; discard marinade. Brush pork with oil. Insert a meat thermometer into thickest portion of pork. Place on a grill rack coated with cooking spray; grill 25 minutes or until thermometer registers 160° (slightly pink). Cut into ¼-inch-thick slices. Sprinkle with cilantro and green onions. Serve with Grilled-Pineapple Salsa. Yield: 8 servings (serving size: 3 ounces pork and ⅓ cup salsa).

CALORIES 194 (26% from fat); FAT 5.6g (sat 1.6g, mono 2.6g, poly 0.7g); PROTEIN 25.5g; CARB 10.5g; FIBER 1.5g; CHOL 79mg; IRON 2.8mg; SODIUM 306mg; CALC 42mg

## Grilled-Pineapple Salsa

1 fresh cored, peeled pineapple, cut into 1-inch slices
1 red bell pepper
1 yellow bell pepper
Cooking spray
½ cup finely chopped red onion
½ cup chopped fresh cilantro
3 tablespoons fresh lime juice
1 tablespoon brown sugar
1½ teaspoons minced crystallized ginger
2 jalapeño peppers, seeded and minced
1 drained canned chipotle chile in adobo sauce, minced

**1.** Preheat grill.
**2.** Place first 3 ingredients on a grill rack coated with cooking spray; grill 3 minutes on each side. Discard stems and seeds from bell peppers; dice pineapple and bell peppers. Combine pineapple, bell pepper, onion, and remaining ingredients; toss gently. Yield: 3 cups (serving size: ⅓ cup).

CALORIES 36 (10% from fat); FAT 0.4g (sat 0g, mono 0.1g, poly 0.1g); PROTEIN 0.6g; CARB 8.7g; FIBER 1.1g; CHOL 0mg; IRON 0.7mg; SODIUM 11mg; CALC 13mg

*Tender, flavorful pork, complemented by the heat and grilled ingredients of the salsa, creates an outstanding combination.*

# Jamaican Jerk Pork Tenderloin

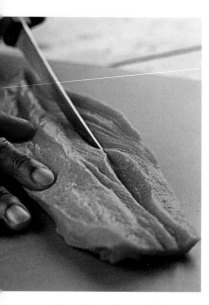

Butterflying the tenderloin will increase the surface area for the marinade to penetrate. After removing the silver skin, simply cut it lengthwise, cutting to, but not all the way through, the other side. Open up the halves; cut each half the same way. Open the pork so that it lies flat, and pour the marinade over the tenderloin. Traditionally, jerk is a dry rub, but you can mix it with liquid to form a paste or marinade as we've done with this recipe. Jerk seasoning is pungent—the longer the meat marinates the more flavorful and spicy it becomes.

2 cups coarsely chopped green onions
½ cup coarsely chopped onion
2 tablespoons white vinegar
1 tablespoon soy sauce
1 tablespoon canola oil
2 teaspoons kosher salt
2 teaspoons thyme sprigs
2 teaspoons brown sugar
2 teaspoons chopped peeled fresh ginger
1 teaspoon ground allspice
¼ teaspoon ground nutmeg
¼ teaspoon black pepper
⅛ teaspoon ground cinnamon
2 garlic cloves, minced
1 to 4 Scotch bonnet or habanero peppers, seeded and chopped
1 (1½-pound) pork tenderloin, trimmed
Cooking spray

**1.** Place first 15 ingredients in a blender or food processor; process until smooth.
**2.** Slice pork lengthwise, cutting to, but not through, other side. Open halves, laying each side flat. Slice each half lengthwise, cutting to, but not through, other side; open flat. Combine pork and green onion mixture in a large zip-top plastic bag. Seal bag; marinate in refrigerator 3 to 24 hours. Remove pork from bag; discard marinade.
**3.** Prepare grill.
**4.** Place pork on a grill rack coated with cooking spray; grill 8 minutes on each side or until meat thermometer registers 160° (slightly pink). Yield: 4 servings (serving size: 3 ounces).

CALORIES 248 (27% from fat); FAT 7.5g (sat 2g, mono 2.8g, poly 2g); PROTEIN 36.9g; CARB 7.1g; FIBER 1.5g; CHOL 111mg; IRON 3.1mg; SODIUM 1,126mg; CALC 52mg

*Pork tenderloin has a mild flavor and is best if enhanced with a spice rub, marinade, or flavorful sauce. The Jamaican jerk marinade is a perfect fit for this selection of meat.*

# Grilled Pork
# Tenderloin Sandwiches

When basting with sugar-based mixtures like the jalapeño jelly used in this recipe, it's important to apply it at just the right time. Basting too early can ruin the flavor of great food. Rather than developing a crusty, sweet caramelized flavor, the sugar burns and chars on the meat creating a bitter, unpalatable flavor.

¼ cup hot jalapeño jelly
1 teaspoon water
1 tablespoon paprika
1½ teaspoons salt
1 teaspoon granulated sugar
1 teaspoon brown sugar
1 teaspoon chili powder
1 teaspoon ground cumin
½ teaspoon freshly ground
   black pepper
2 (1-pound) pork tenderloins,
   trimmed
Cooking spray
¼ cup light ranch dressing
¼ cup sweet hickory smoke
   tomato-based barbecue
   sauce (such as Bull's-Eye)
8 (1½-ounce) hamburger buns
   or Kaiser rolls

1. Prepare grill.
2. Combine jelly and water; set aside.
3. Combine paprika and next 6 ingredients; rub evenly over pork. Place pork on a grill rack coated with cooking spray; cover and grill 15 minutes, turning pork occasionally. Brush pork with jelly mixture. Grill 5 minutes or until thermometer registers 160° (slightly pink).
4. Place pork on a cutting surface. Cover loosely with foil; let stand 10 minutes. Cut pork into thin slices. Combine ranch dressing and barbecue sauce. Serve pork and ranch mixture with buns. Yield: 8 servings (serving size: 1 bun, 3 ounces pork, and 1 tablespoon sauce).

CALORIES 329 (22% from fat); FAT 8g (sat 2g, mono 2.1g, poly 1.6g); PROTEIN 27.8g; CARB 34.6g; FIBER 1.8g; CHOL 76mg; IRON 3.1mg; SODIUM 920mg; CALC 73mg

*For an easy, on-the-go meal, prepare the pork and assemble the sandwiches at home. Simply wrap them in aluminum foil, and they'll stay warm while you travel. Or slice and refrigerate roasted tenderloin, and serve the sandwiches cold. Take along the dressing, and allow everyone to put together their own sandwiches.*

# Pork Kebabs with Guava Sauce

Guava paste is made from the pulp and juice of the tropical guava fruit. The pulp and juice are combined with sugar, pectin, and citric acid, then cooked slowly to form a rich, thick paste. The sweet-sour flavor of the paste can be used as a base for sauces or sliced and served with cheese. Guava paste is sold in Latin markets and large supermarkets in a 16-ounce package. Store any unused product in the refrigerator because it's easier to cut when chilled.

**Pork:**
  1 tablespoon ground oregano
  1½ teaspoons olive oil
  ¾ teaspoon salt
  ½ teaspoon freshly ground
    black pepper
  2½ pounds boneless pork loin,
    cut into 1½-inch cubes
  2 large onions, each cut into
    16 wedges
Cooking spray
**Sauce:**
  1 cup chopped commercial
    guava paste (about 12
    ounces)
  ½ cup less-sodium beef broth
  2 tablespoons fresh lime juice
  2 tablespoons dark rum
  ¼ teaspoon salt

**1.** To prepare pork, combine first 4 ingredients in a large bowl. Add pork; stir to coat. Cover and refrigerate 2 hours.
**2.** Thread pork and onion alternately onto 16 (8-inch) skewers.
**3.** Prepare grill.
**4.** Place skewers on a grill rack coated with cooking spray, and grill 14 minutes or until done, turning occasionally. Arrange skewers on a serving platter; keep warm.
**5.** To prepare sauce, combine guava paste and remaining 4 ingredients in a small saucepan. Bring to a simmer over medium heat; cook 8 minutes or until smooth, stirring constantly. Serve sauce with pork. Yield: 8 servings (serving size: 2 kebabs and about 2½ tablespoons sauce).
**Note:** If using wooden skewers, soak them in water 30 minutes before grilling.

CALORIES 357 (22% from fat); FAT 8.6g (sat 2.8g, mono 4.1g, poly 1g); PROTEIN 31.7g; CARB 34.2g; FIBER 1.3g; CHOL 78mg; IRON 1.5mg; SODIUM 361mg; CALC 47mg

*Oregano gives this pork dish great flavor. Add a tossed green salad, and you've got a meal. Slice the remaining guava paste, and serve it as an appetizer with queso fresco cheese and crackers.*

# Fennel-Brined Pork Chops

It's very important to pat the pork chops dry with a paper towel before grilling. Excess moisture will keep the chops from browning. Because the chops are thin and cook quickly, be careful not to overcook the chops while waiting for the characteristic brown grill marks to appear.

3½ cups water, divided
½ cup chopped fennel fronds
1 tablespoon fennel seeds
¼ cup kosher salt
¼ cup sugar
2 tablespoons sambuca or other anise-flavored liqueur
1 cup ice cubes
4 (4-ounce) boneless center-cut loin pork chops (about ¾ inch thick)
Cooking spray
2 teaspoons chopped fresh rosemary
1 teaspoon freshly ground black pepper
2 garlic cloves, minced

**1.** Combine 1 cup water, fennel fronds, and seeds in a small saucepan. Bring to a boil; remove from heat. Pour into a large bowl; cool to room temperature. Add 2½ cups water, salt, sugar, and liqueur, stirring until salt and sugar dissolve. Pour salt mixture into a large zip-top plastic bag. Add ice and pork; seal. Refrigerate 4 hours, turning bag occasionally.

**2.** Prepare grill.

**3.** Remove pork from bag; discard brine. Pat pork dry with paper towels. Coat pork with cooking spray. Combine rosemary, pepper, and garlic; rub evenly over both sides of pork. Place pork on a grill rack coated with cooking spray; grill 3 to 5 minutes on each side or until done. Let stand 5 minutes before serving. Yield: 4 servings (serving size: 1 chop).

CALORIES 174 (34% from fat); FAT 6.5g (sat 2.4g, mono 2.9g, poly 0.5g); PROTEIN 24.1g; CARB 3g; FIBER 0.3g; CHOL 65mg; IRON 0.9mg; SODIUM 469mg; CALC 34mg

*Brining is simply a matter of soaking meat in a saltwater solution, yet the result is the difference between dry and delicious. Unlike marinating, which imparts flavor, brining enhances texture. The process locks in moisture so that the end product is always a succulent, juicy piece of pork or chicken.*

# Grilled Plum and Prosciutto-Stuffed Pork Chops

Boneless loin pork chops are excellent for stuffing. Use a thin-bladed knife to cut a horizontal slit through the thickest portion of the chop to form a pocket. Cut to, but not through, the other side of the chop. Get a head start by assembling the stuffed pork chops the night before. Placing the prosciutto wrap in the pocket overnight will allow the flavors to permeate throughout the pork chops. Sprinkle them with the fennel mixture just prior to grilling.

4 pitted dried plums, halved
2 very thin slices prosciutto (about ¾ ounce), halved
½ teaspoon crushed fennel seeds
½ teaspoon paprika
½ teaspoon chopped fresh sage
½ teaspoon chopped fresh rosemary
¼ teaspoon kosher salt
¼ teaspoon crushed red pepper
¼ teaspoon freshly ground black pepper
4 (4-ounce) boneless center-cut loin pork chops (about ¾ inch thick)
Cooking spray
2 teaspoons balsamic vinegar
2 teaspoons molasses

1. Prepare grill.
2. Soak plum halves in boiling water 5 minutes. Drain.
3. Wrap 2 plum halves in each prosciutto piece.
4. Combine fennel seeds and next 6 ingredients in a small bowl.
5. Cut a horizontal slit through thickest portion of each pork chop to form a pocket. Stuff 1 prosciutto wrap into each pocket. Sprinkle pork chops with fennel mixture. Place pork chops on a grill rack coated with cooking spray; grill 3 to 5 minutes on each side or until done. Combine vinegar and molasses; brush over pork chops. Yield: 4 servings (serving size: 1 chop).

CALORIES 205 (32% from fat); FAT 7.2g (sat 2.6g, mono 2.9g, poly 0.5g); PROTEIN 25.7g; CARB 8.5g; FIBER 0.9g; CHOL 70mg; IRON 1.3mg; SODIUM 270mg; CALC 42mg

*The flavors of chopped green onion, minced garlic, and white hominy sautéed in butter create a delicious side dish for the pork chops.*

# Grilled Pork Chops with Tomatillo, Corn, and Avocado Salsa

Tomatillos are an apple-green fruit with tangy flavor and a papery husk that splits open as the fruit matures. Grilling tomatillos enhances their natural tartness and softens their tough skin.

**Salsa:**
- ¾ pound tomatillos
- 1 ear shucked corn
- Cooking spray
- ¼ cup finely chopped red onion
- 3 tablespoons chopped fresh cilantro
- 2 tablespoons fresh lime juice
- 1 tablespoon minced seeded jalapeño pepper
- ¼ teaspoon salt
- ⅛ teaspoon freshly ground black pepper
- 1 garlic clove, minced
- ½ cup diced peeled avocado

**Pork:**
- 6 (6-ounce) bone-in loin pork chops (about 1 inch thick)
- 1 teaspoon freshly ground black pepper
- ½ teaspoon salt

**1.** Prepare grill.

**2.** To prepare salsa, discard husks and stems from tomatillos. Place tomatillos and corn on a grill rack coated with cooking spray; grill 10 minutes or until browned, turning tomatillos and corn occasionally. Place tomatillos in a food processor; process until smooth. Cut kernels from ear of corn. Combine tomatillo puree, corn, onion, and next 6 ingredients in a medium bowl; gently stir in avocado just before serving.

**3.** To prepare pork, sprinkle pork with 1 teaspoon black pepper and ½ teaspoon salt. Place pork on a grill rack coated with cooking spray; grill 5 minutes on each side or until done. Serve pork with salsa. Yield: 6 servings (serving size: 1 pork chop and ⅓ cup salsa).

CALORIES 235 (37% from fat); FAT 9.6g (sat 2.9g, mono 4.4g, poly 1.1g); PROTEIN 27.2g; CARB 10.4g; FIBER 2.7g; CHOL 69mg; IRON 1.5mg; SODIUM 350mg; CALC 37mg

*To make this quick-and-easy recipe even easier, prepare the salsa the day before and refrigerate. The pork chop and salsa are delicious served over basmati rice with a side of jícama and carrot slaw.*

# Grilled Pork Chops with Rhubarb Chutney

Rhubarb is an ancient plant whose medicinal uses and horticulture have been recorded in history since ancient China. Today, this tart plant can be bought by the bunch in the produce section of your local grocery store. Hothouse-grown rhubarb is available in some areas almost year-round; field-grown rhubarb's peak season is April through June. The thick, celery-like stalks are the only edible portion of the plant. Wash and remove the leaves just before using.

**Chutney:**
- ½ cup sugar
- ¼ cup balsamic vinegar
- ¼ teaspoon ground coriander
- 1 (3-inch) cinnamon stick
- 2 cups coarsely chopped rhubarb (about ½ pound)
- ⅓ cup dried cranberries
- ¼ cup chopped green onions
- ¼ teaspoon salt
- ¼ teaspoon ground red pepper

**Pork:**
- ⅓ cup red currant jelly
- 1 tablespoon whole-grain Dijon mustard
- ½ teaspoon salt
- ½ teaspoon black pepper
- ¼ teaspoon ground cumin
- 4 (6-ounce) bone-in center-cut pork chops (about ¼ inch thick)

Cooking spray
Thinly sliced green onions (optional)

**1.** To prepare chutney, combine first 4 ingredients in a small saucepan. Bring to a boil over medium-high heat. Add rhubarb and next 4 ingredients; reduce heat. Simmer 5 minutes or until rhubarb is tender. Spoon into a bowl; cover. Chill at least 2 hours. Discard cinnamon stick.

**2.** Prepare grill.

**3.** To prepare pork, combine jelly and mustard in a small bowl; set aside.

**4.** Combine ½ teaspoon salt, black pepper, and cumin; rub evenly over pork. Place pork on a grill rack coated with cooking spray; grill 4 minutes on each side or until done, basting occasionally with jelly mixture. Serve pork with chutney; sprinkle with sliced green onions, if desired. Yield: 4 servings (serving size: 1 pork chop and ½ cup chutney).

CALORIES 400 (16% from fat); FAT 7g (sat 2.5g, mono 3.1g, poly 0.6g); PROTEIN 26.2g; CARB 55.9g; FIBER 2.6g; CHOL 69mg; IRON 1.2mg; SODIUM 596mg; CALC 89mg

*A simple jelly-and-mustard glaze coats pork chops that are topped with a sweet-tart chutney. Serve with rice or couscous to soak up the sauce.*

# poultry

# Beer-Can Chicken with Cola Barbecue Sauce

While American ingenuity has produced a variety of beer-can roasters that hold the can in place and stabilize the tipsy chicken, a special roaster isn't needed for this recipe. Instead, use the beer can as the third leg of a tripod; spread the drumsticks out to support the chicken. The flavors of the hickory wood chips and spice rub permeate the chicken from the outside. The beer infuses the chicken with flavor from the inside. The results will convince you that this unique cooking method is worth the effort.

**Chicken:**
- 1 (12-ounce) can beer
- 1 cup hickory wood chips
- 2 teaspoons kosher or sea salt
- 2 teaspoons brown sugar
- 2 teaspoons sweet paprika
- 1 teaspoon coarsely ground black pepper
- 1 (4-pound) whole chicken
- Cooking spray

**Sauce:**
- ½ cup cola
- ½ cup ketchup
- 2 tablespoons Worcestershire sauce
- 1½ teaspoons steak sauce (such as A1)
- ½ teaspoon liquid smoke
- ½ teaspoon instant onion flakes
- ½ teaspoon instant minced garlic
- ¼ teaspoon black pepper

**1.** To prepare chicken, open beer can. Carefully pierce top of beer can with "church-key" can opener several times; set aside. Soak wood chips in water 1 hour. Combine salt, sugar, paprika, and 1 teaspoon pepper; set aside.

**2.** To prepare grill for indirect grilling, place a disposable aluminum foil pan in center of grill. Arrange charcoal around foil pan; heat to medium heat.

**3.** Remove and discard giblets and neck from chicken. Rinse chicken with cold water; pat dry. Trim excess fat. Starting at neck cavity, loosen skin from breast and drumsticks by inserting fingers, gently pushing between skin and meat.

**4.** Rub 2 teaspoons spice mixture under loosened skin. Rub 2 teaspoons spice mixture in body cavity. Rub 2 teaspoons spice mixture over skin. Slowly add remaining spice mixture to beer can (salt will make beer foam). Holding chicken upright with body cavity facing down, insert beer can into cavity.

**5.** Drain wood chips. Place half of wood chips on hot coals. Coat grill rack with cooking spray. Place chicken on grill rack over drip pan. Spread legs out to form a tripod to support chicken. Cover and grill 2 hours or until a meat thermometer inserted into meaty portion of thigh registers 180°. Add remaining wood chips after 1 hour and charcoal as needed.

**6.** Lift chicken slightly using tongs; place spatula under can. Carefully lift chicken and can; place on a cutting board. Let stand 5 minutes. Gently lift chicken using tongs or insulated rubber gloves; carefully twist can, and remove from cavity. Discard skin and can.

**7.** To prepare sauce, combine cola and remaining 7 ingredients in a saucepan; bring to a boil. Reduce heat, and simmer 6 minutes. Cool. Serve with chicken. Yield: 6 servings (serving size: 3 ounces chicken and about 2 tablespoons sauce).

CALORIES 215 (20% from fat); FAT 4.7g (sat 1.1g, mono 1.4g, poly 1.3g); PROTEIN 31.8g; CARB 10g; FIBER 0.5g; CHOL 100mg; IRON 2.2mg; SODIUM 741mg; CALC 29mg

# Rum-Marinated Chicken Breasts with Pineapple Relish

A clean grill is particularly important when grilling fruit such as fresh pineapple. We recommend cleaning your grill twice: once after preheating the grill, and again when you've finished grilling. Use both a metal spatula and a wire brush to scrape the grates clean, and coat the grill rack with cooking spray to keep the food from sticking.

**Chicken:**
- ½ cup dark rum
- ¼ cup barbecue sauce
- 3 tablespoons fresh lime juice
- 1 tablespoon Caribbean hot sauce (such as Pickapeppa Sauce)
- 1 teaspoon sea or kosher salt
- 2 teaspoons canola oil
- 4 (8-ounce) bone-in chicken breast halves

**Relish:**
- 1 small pineapple, peeled, cored, and cut into ½-inch-thick rings (about 12 ounces)
- Cooking spray
- ½ cup finely chopped red bell pepper
- 1 teaspoon grated lime rind
- 2 tablespoons fresh lime juice
- 1 teaspoon dark rum
- ¼ teaspoon Caribbean hot sauce
- ⅛ teaspoon sea or kosher salt
- 8 lime slices

**1.** To prepare chicken, combine first 6 ingredients in large zip-top plastic bag. Add chicken to bag; seal. Marinate in refrigerator 1 to 2 hours, turning bag occasionally. Remove chicken from bag, reserving marinade; set chicken aside. Let marinade stand at room temperature 10 minutes. Strain through a sieve into a bowl; discard solids. Set marinade aside.

**2.** Prepare grill.

**3.** To prepare relish, place pineapple on a grill rack coated with cooking spray; grill 3 minutes on each side or until soft and browned around the edge. Cool slightly; chop. Combine pineapple, bell pepper, and next 5 ingredients; set aside.

**4.** Place chicken on grill rack coated with cooking spray; grill 30 minutes or until done, turning occasionally. Remove and discard skin.

**5.** Bring reserved marinade to a boil in a small saucepan; cook 1 minute. Drizzle cooked marinade over chicken. Serve chicken with relish and lime wedges. Yield: 4 servings (serving size: 1 chicken breast half, ½ cup relish, 2 tablespoons sauce, and 2 lime slices).

CALORIES 289 (14% from fat); FAT 4.5g (sat 0.5g, mono 2.2g, poly 0.9g); PROTEIN 29.6g; CARB 15.6g; FIBER 1.9g; CHOL 72mg; IRON 1.5mg; SODIUM 971mg; CALC 28mg

*The skin helps keep chicken moist while grilling and can be easily removed before serving or at the table. Keep the thinner edges of the breast toward the cooler edge of the fire. The chicken is done when the juices near the bone run clear.*

# Jerk Chicken

This method of cooking dates back to the Carib-Arawak Indians who inhabited Jamaica. The meat was "jerked" or pierced with a sharp object, creating holes which were stuffed with various spices. Then the meat was placed on hot stones in a deep pit and covered with green wood to slow cook. Today chicken and pork are simply dry-rubbed with a spicy mixture called Jamaican jerk spice or jerk sauce and grilled. While the chicken looks charred, it's the jerk sauce and ketchup that create the rich mahogany color.

1 cup vertically sliced onion
¼ cup fresh lemon juice
¼ cup jerk sauce
¼ teaspoon salt
¼ teaspoon black pepper
3 garlic cloves, chopped
4 bone-in chicken breast
 halves (about 1½ pounds),
 skinned
4 bone-in chicken thighs
 (about 1 pound), skinned
½ cup light beer
¼ cup jerk sauce
3 tablespoons ketchup
1 tablespoon hot sauce
Cooking spray
Julienne-cut green onions
 (optional)

**1.** Combine first 6 ingredients in a large zip-top plastic bag. Add chicken to bag; seal. Marinate in refrigerator overnight, turning occasionally. Remove chicken from bag; discard marinade.
**2.** Prepare grill.
**3.** Combine beer, ¼ cup jerk sauce, ketchup, and hot sauce.
**4.** Place chicken on grill rack coated with cooking spray; grill 20 minutes or until done, turning and basting frequently with beer mixture. Garnish chicken with green onions, if desired. Yield: 6 servings (serving size: about 4 ounces).

CALORIES 198 (21% from fat); FAT 4.6g (sat 1.3g, mono 1.6g, poly 1.1g); PROTEIN 26.2g; CARB 10.1g; FIBER 0.2g; CHOL 75mg; IRON 1.1mg; SODIUM 539mg; CALC 18mg

*For a change of pace from basic grilled chicken, try this spicy recipe. Adjust the heat by adding more or less hot sauce to satisfy your taste preferences. If there happens to be any leftovers, jerk chicken makes delicious sandwiches.*

# Grilled Herb-Coated Chicken Breasts

¾ cup Herbed Lemon-
    Buttermilk Dressing
4 (4-ounce) skinless, boneless
    chicken breast halves
½ teaspoon salt
½ teaspoon freshly ground
    black pepper
2 tablespoons finely chopped
    fresh parsley
2 tablespoons finely chopped
    fresh chives
1 teaspoon canola oil
1 teaspoon honey
Cooking spray

**1.** Combine Herbed Lemon-Buttermilk Dressing and chicken in a large zip-top plastic bag. Seal and marinate in refrigerator 1 hour or up to 8 hours, turning bag occasionally.
**2.** Prepare grill.
**3.** Remove chicken from marinade; discard marinade. Sprinkle evenly with salt and pepper. Combine parsley, chives, oil, and honey, stirring well. Spoon herb mixture evenly over tops of chicken. Place chicken, herb side down, on a grill rack coated with cooking spray; grill 8 minutes each side or until done. Yield: 4 servings (serving size: 1 chicken breast half).

(Totals include Herbed Lemon-Buttermilk Dressing) CALORIES 169 (24% from fat); FAT 4.6g (sat 0.9g, mono 1g, poly 0.7g); PROTEIN 26.9g; CARB 3.4g; FIBER 0.3g; CHOL 68mg; IRON 1mg; SODIUM 481mg; CALC 37mg

Chives vary in shape from grass-fine to pencil-thick. The thicker the chive, the more flavor it packs. In order to chop chives safely, hold chives in a bunch and place on a clean cutting board. With a sharp knife chop chives to desired size. Keep in the refrigerator until they're ready to be used. The coating of chopped herbs on the tender chicken breast provides protection from the hot grill as well as subtle flavor.

## Herbed Lemon-Buttermilk Dressing

¾ cup fat-free buttermilk
⅓ cup low-fat mayonnaise
1 tablespoon grated lemon rind
1 tablespoon chopped onion
2 teaspoons fresh lemon juice
2 teaspoons Dijon mustard
1 teaspoon finely chopped
    fresh chives
1 teaspoon finely chopped
    fresh basil
1 teaspoon finely chopped
    fresh thyme
½ teaspoon coarsely ground
    black pepper
¼ teaspoon salt
1 garlic clove, minced

**1.** Combine all ingredients, stirring with a whisk until well blended. Yield: 1¼ cups (serving size: 1 tablespoon).
**Note:** Refrigerate dressing in an airtight container up to five days; stir well before using.

CALORIES 18 (65% from fat); FAT 1.3g (sat 0.3g, mono 0g, poly 0g); PROTEIN 0.4g; CARB 1g; FIBER 0.1g; CHOL 1mg; IRON 0mg; SODIUM 77mg; CALC 13mg

*This all-purpose dressing is similar to ranch dressing and is great as a marinade on chicken. The longer it marinates, the tastier and moister the end product. Serve the chicken breast with mixed greens and additional dressing.*

# Sizzling Chicken Fajitas

When slicing onions, start at the end opposite the root. Onions contain sulfuric compounds that are released when they are peeled or sliced. Those compounds irritate the eyes and produce tears. Since more of these compounds are found in the root, it's best to cut that last. Slice the top off the onion, leaving the root end intact. Remove the papery skin, and slice the onion in half vertically. Continue cutting the onion vertically into thin slices.

½ cup low-sodium soy sauce
⅓ cup water
⅓ cup white vinegar
¼ teaspoon garlic powder
¼ teaspoon black pepper
1½ pounds skinless, boneless
    chicken breast
Cooking spray
1 tablespoon canola oil
1 cup green bell pepper strips
    (about 1 medium)
1 cup red bell pepper strips
    (about 1 medium)
1 cup vertically sliced red
    onion
1 teaspoon seasoned salt
6 (8-inch) fat-free flour tortillas
¾ cup bottled salsa
¾ cup fat-free sour cream

**1.** Combine first 5 ingredients; reserve ¼ cup soy sauce mixture. Combine remaining mixture and chicken in a large zip-top plastic bag. Seal and marinate in refrigerator 3 hours, turning occasionally.
**2.** Prepare grill.
**3.** Remove chicken from marinade; discard marinade. Place chicken on a grill rack coated with cooking spray; cover and grill 10 minutes on each side or until done.
**4.** Heat oil in a large nonstick skillet over medium-high heat. Add bell peppers and onion; sprinkle with seasoned salt. Sauté 4 minutes or until tender. Add reserved soy sauce mixture, and cook 2 minutes. Cut chicken into thin slices; add to vegetable mixture.
**5.** Warm tortillas according to package directions. Keep chicken warm in skillet while preparing tortilla. Serve chicken mixture immediately with warm tortillas, salsa, and sour cream. Yield: 6 servings (serving size: 1 cup chicken mixture, 2 tablespoons salsa, 2 tablespoons sour cream, and 1 tortilla).

CALORIES 353 (11% from fat); FAT 4.4g (sat 0.6g, mono 1.7g, poly 1.1g); PROTEIN 33.9g; CARB 41.9g; FIBER 3.4g; CHOL 71mg; IRON 1.2mg; SODIUM 1,366mg; CALC 90mg

*Sometimes the best fajitas are homemade. And these truly stack up to any local Mexican restaurant's best. Easy to prepare and packed with flavor, this recipe is one you'll turn to every time you get a craving for authentic fajita fare.*

# Grilled Chicken Salad with Feta and Orange Vinaigrette

Perk up green salads by "going orange" with products you can keep on hand. Frozen orange concentrate adds a sweet tanginess to a basic vinaigrette that far surpasses the flavor you get in bottled vinaigrettes. Tender mandarin oranges can transform a ho-hum green salad into something special by adding a sweet contrast to the greens and vegetables.

1 pound skinless, boneless chicken breast
Cooking spray
8 cups torn leaf lettuce
1 cup orange bell pepper strips
1 cup grape or cherry tomatoes, halved
½ cup matchstick-cut carrots
½ cup (2 ounces) feta cheese, crumbled
¼ cup chopped green onions
3 tablespoons thawed orange juice concentrate, undiluted
1 tablespoon white vinegar
1 tablespoon olive oil
⅛ teaspoon salt
⅛ teaspoon black pepper
1 (11-ounce) can mandarin oranges in light syrup, drained
2 tablespoons sliced almonds, toasted

**1.** Prepare grill.
**2.** Place chicken on a grill rack coated with cooking spray; grill 6 minutes on each side or until done. Cut chicken into ½-inch-thick slices. Set aside.
**3.** Combine lettuce and next 5 ingredients in a large bowl. Combine orange juice concentrate, vinegar, oil, salt, and black pepper; stir with a whisk. Pour juice mixture over lettuce mixture, tossing to coat. Place lettuce mixture on each of 4 plates; top with chicken, oranges, and almonds. Yield: 4 servings (serving size: about 2 cups lettuce mixture, 3 ounces chicken, about 10 mandarin orange segments, and 1½ teaspoons almonds).

CALORIES 299 (28% from fat); FAT 9.3g (sat 3g, mono 4.4g, poly 1.2g); PROTEIN 25.1g; CARB 31.2g; FIBER 4.8g; CHOL 62mg; IRON 1.5mg; SODIUM 351mg; CALC 161mg

*A great way to use grilled chicken is in a fresh green salad. In this one, the sweetness of orange and bell pepper is a pleasing contrast to the tanginess of feta cheese and the orange vinaigrette.*

# Grilled Chicken Mojito Sandwiches

The Cuban Mojito (moh-HEE-toh) is a popular cocktail containing fresh lime juice, mint, and rum. Combine these ingredients with a little garlic and you have a quick marinade for chicken tenders.

**Dressing:**

¼ cup light mayonnaise
¼ teaspoon finely grated lime rind
3 tablespoons minced fresh mint
1 tablespoon fresh lime juice
1 teaspoon sugar
1 teaspoon minced serrano chile (with seeds)

**Sandwiches:**

1 tablespoon minced fresh mint
3 tablespoons fresh lime juice
2 tablespoons dark rum
1 teaspoon ground cumin
1 garlic clove, crushed
1 pound chicken breast tenders
4 (¼-inch-thick) slices Vidalia or other sweet onion
Cooking spray
¼ teaspoon salt
¼ teaspoon freshly ground black pepper
4 (2-ounce) French rolls, halved
8 (¼-inch-thick) slices tomato
4 red leaf lettuce leaves

**1.** To prepare dressing, combine first 6 ingredients in a small bowl, stirring with a whisk. Cover and chill.

**2.** To prepare sandwiches, combine 1 tablespoon mint and next 4 ingredients in a large zip-top plastic bag. Add chicken breast tenders; seal and marinate in refrigerator 15 minutes, turning occasionally.

**3.** Prepare grill.

**4.** Remove chicken from bag; discard marinade. Place chicken and onion on a grill rack coated with cooking spray. Grill 4 minutes on each side or until chicken is done and onion is tender. Remove chicken and onion from grill; sprinkle chicken with salt and pepper.

**5.** Grill roll halves, cut sides down, about 1 minute or until lightly toasted. Spread about 1 tablespoon dressing over bottom halves of rolls.

**6.** Top each serving with 3 ounces chicken breast tenders, 1 onion slice, 2 tomato slices, and 1 lettuce leaf; cover with top halves of rolls. Yield: 4 servings (serving size: 1 sandwich).

CALORIES 375 (22% from fat); FAT 9.1g (sat 2g, mono 1.5g, poly 0.9g); PROTEIN 32.2g; CARB 37.7g; FIBER 3.3g; CHOL 71mg; IRON 3mg; SODIUM 693mg; CALC 90mg

*Chicken tenders are ideal for sandwiches because the small pieces fit nicely on rolls and buns. Since the tenders are small and can easily slip through the grill rack, you can use a grill basket to cook the chicken and onion slices.*

# Grilled Chicken Kebabs

1 cup Pomegranate-Orange
  Dressing, divided
2 pounds skinless, boneless
  chicken thighs, trimmed and
  cut into bite-sized pieces
2 large oranges
¼ teaspoon salt
¼ teaspoon black pepper
Cooking spray
¼ cup chopped fresh mint

**1.** Combine ½ cup Pomegranate-Orange Dressing and chicken in a large zip-top plastic bag. Seal and marinate in refrigerator 30 minutes, turning bag occasionally.
**2.** Prepare grill.
**3.** Cut each orange into 8 wedges; cut each wedge crosswise into 3 pieces.
**4.** Remove chicken from marinade; discard marinade. Thread chicken and orange alternately onto 16 (10-inch) skewers. Sprinkle with salt and pepper. Place kebabs on a grill rack coated with cooking spray; grill 5 minutes on each side or until chicken is done, basting occasionally with remaining ½ cup Pomegranate-Orange Dressing. Sprinkle with mint. Yield: 8 servings (serving size: 2 kebabs).
**Note:** If using wooden skewers, soak them in water 30 minutes before grilling.

(Totals include Pomegranate-Orange Dressing) CALORIES 205 (35% from fat); FAT 8g (sat 1.6g, mono 4.1g, poly 1.4g); PROTEIN 22.7g; CARB 9g; FIBER 0.7g; CHOL 94mg; IRON 1.6mg; SODIUM 320mg; CALC 35mg

Pomegranate molasses is a syrupy sour-sweet juice reduction often used in Middle Eastern cuisine to intensify the flavors of sauces and marinades, as in this recipe. It's also used in soups and stews or for braising meats and fish. The sweetness comes mainly from the concentration of the fruit's natural sugars, not from added sugar. You can find it in bottles in Middle Eastern markets and some specialty shops.

# Pomegranate-Orange Dressing

1 cup fresh orange juice
2½ tablespoons balsamic vinegar
2 tablespoons fresh lemon juice
2 tablespoons pomegranate
  molasses
2 teaspoons grated orange rind
2 teaspoons minced rosemary
1 teaspoon salt
1 teaspoon brown sugar
½ teaspoon ground cumin
½ teaspoon ground black pepper
¼ teaspoon ground red pepper
4 garlic cloves, minced
¼ cup extravirgin olive oil

**1.** Combine all ingredients except oil, stirring with a whisk. Gradually add oil, stirring constantly with a whisk until well combined. Yield: about 1½ cups (serving size: 1 tablespoon).
**Note:** Refrigerate dressing in an airtight container up to five days; stir well before using.

CALORIES 39 (55% from fat); FAT 2.4g (sat 0.3g, mono 1.8g, poly 0.2g); PROTEIN 0.1g; CARB 4.1g; FIBER 0.1g; CHOL 0mg; IRON 0.3mg; SODIUM 99mg; CALC 9mg

*The dark meat of chicken thighs stands up to the strong flavors of the marinade. If you have any leftover dressing, serve it as a dipping sauce.*

# Grilled Cornish Hens with Apricot-Mustard Glaze

Cornish hens are a special breed of small chickens with short legs and broad breasts. They're usually sold frozen in supermarkets and must be thawed before cooking. Look for the smallest ones you can find—they'll be the most tender and have the best flavor. Remove the skin and quarter the hens before grilling. The apricot glaze will protect the meat and keep it moist.

½ cup apricot preserves
¼ cup stone-ground mustard
2 tablespoons chopped fresh flat-leaf parsley
2 tablespoons chopped fresh mint
2 teaspoons Champagne vinegar or white wine vinegar
2 (18-ounce) Cornish hens, skinned and quartered
¼ teaspoon kosher salt
½ teaspoon freshly ground black pepper
Cooking spray

**1.** Combine first 5 ingredients, stirring with a whisk.
**2.** Sprinkle hens with salt and pepper. Place ¼ cup apricot mixture in a large zip-top plastic bag. Add hens; seal and marinate in refrigerator 1 hour, turning bag occasionally.
**3.** Prepare grill.
**4.** Remove hens from bag; discard marinade. Place hens on a grill rack coated with cooking spray; grill 12 minutes or until thermometer registers 180°, turning hens occasionally and basting frequently with remaining apricot mixture. Yield: 2 servings (serving size: 1 hen).

CALORIES 417 (15% from fat); FAT 7g (sat 1.7g, mono 2.2g, poly 1.6g); PROTEIN 41.7g; CARB 44.6g; FIBER 3.7g; CHOL 180mg; IRON 2.3mg; SODIUM 608mg; CALC 70mg

*Serve the hens with grilled fennel bulb quarters and cous-cous. Preserves are chunkier than jelly and thus adhere better to the Cornish hens; peach preserves are a tasty alternative to the apricot preserves used in this recipe.*

# Turkey Burgers with Goat Cheese

3 pounds lean ground turkey
3 tablespoons chopped fresh parsley
1 tablespoon chopped fresh rosemary
¼ teaspoon kosher salt
¼ teaspoon freshly ground black pepper
Cooking spray
8 (1½-ounce) hamburger buns
4 ounces goat cheese, cut into 8 slices

**1.** Prepare grill.
**2.** Combine first 5 ingredients in a large bowl. Divide turkey mixture into 8 equal portions, shaping each into a ½-inch-thick patty. Place patties on a grill rack coated with cooking spray; cook 5 minutes on each side or until done. Place buns, cut sides down, on grill rack; cook 1 minute or until lightly browned. Place patties on bottom halves of buns. Top each patty with 1 slice goat cheese. Cover with top halves of buns. Yield: 8 servings (serving size: 1 burger).

CALORIES 336 (19% from fat); FAT 7.1g (sat 2.5g, mono 1.1g, poly 1g); PROTEIN 48.2g; CARB 22.2g; FIBER 1.2g; CHOL 74mg; IRON 3.5mg; SODIUM 466mg; CALC 60mg

Not all ground turkey is created equal. Regular ground turkey (labeled 85% lean) is a combination of white and dark meat, which is comparable to some lean cuts of ground beef. Frozen ground turkey, which is all dark meat and can contain skin, can be just as high in fat as regular ground beef. Ground turkey breast is the lowest in fat (up to 99% lean), but it can dry out easily when grilled. For optimum flavor and texture, avoid pressing down on these burgers with a spatula as they grill.

## Grilled Pepper Relish

4 bell peppers (assorted colors, such as red, yellow, and orange)
¼ cup chopped fresh basil
2 tablespoons chopped pitted kalamata olives
1 tablespoon balsamic vinegar
1 teaspoon chopped fresh thyme
1½ teaspoons olive oil
¼ teaspoon salt
¼ teaspoon black pepper

**1.** Prepare grill.
**2.** Place bell peppers on grill rack. Grill, without lid, 5 to 7 minutes, turning frequently, until peppers blister. Place peppers in a zip-top plastic bag; seal. Let stand 15 minutes. Peel peppers; remove and discard seeds. Cut peppers into ½-inch pieces.
**3.** Combine bell peppers and remaining ingredients in a medium bowl; toss well. Yield: 8 servings (serving size: ¼ cup).

CALORIES 39 (55% from fat); FAT 2.4g (sat 0.3g, mono 1.8g, poly 0.2g); PROTEIN 0.1g; CARB 4.1g; FIBER 0.1g; CHOL 0mg; IRON 0.3mg; SODIUM 99mg; CALC 9mg

*Turkey burgers are a low fat and delicious alternative to ground beef. Like regular hamburgers, they're shaped into patties and can be cooked on the grill or stove, or cooked in the oven. Top the burgers with Grilled Pepper Relish for some extra zing if you prefer.*

# fish &
# shellfish

# Peppered Halibut Fillets

Halibut, a white and mild-flavored fish, comes in steaks and fillets. Although it's a firm fish, it's a little more delicate than grouper, sea bass, or mahimahi, so be gentle when turning it on the grill.

1 tablespoon coarsely ground
    black pepper
1 tablespoon fresh lemon juice
1½ teaspoons canola oil
4 (6-ounce) halibut fillets
¾ teaspoon sea or kosher salt
Cooking spray
4 lemon wedges

**1.** Prepare grill.
**2.** Combine first 3 ingredients; rub over fish. Cover, and let stand at room temperature 10 minutes. Sprinkle fish with salt.
**3.** Place fish on a grill rack coated with cooking spray; grill 4 minutes on each side or until fish flakes easily when tested with a fork. Serve with lemon wedges. Yield: 4 servings (serving size: 1 fillet and 1 lemon wedge).

CALORIES 210 (24% from fat); FAT 5.7g (sat 0.7g, mono 2.3g, poly 1.8g); PROTEIN 35.6g; CARB 1.9g; FIBER 0.4g; CHOL 54mg; IRON 1.5mg; SODIUM 524mg; CALC 87mg

*Serve these lightly peppered fillets with steamed asparagus and a lemon wedge to add vibrant color to your plate. A side of fluffy, brown rice would be a nice addition as well.*

# Grilled Salmon with East-West Spice Rub and Orange-Soy Glaze

**Spice Mixture:**
- 1 tablespoon sugar
- 1½ teaspoons five-spice powder
- 1½ teaspoons ground coriander
- 1½ teaspoons black pepper
- ½ teaspoon salt

**Glaze:**
- 3 (3 x ½–inch) orange rind strips
- ½ cup fresh orange juice
- ½ cup low-sodium soy sauce
- ⅓ cup honey
- 2 tablespoons minced green onions
- 1 tablespoon minced peeled fresh ginger
- 1½ teaspoons dark sesame oil
- 4 garlic cloves, minced
- 1 (3-inch) cinnamon stick

**Fish:**
- 8 (6-ounce) salmon fillets (about 2 inches thick)
- Cooking spray
- ¼ cup thinly sliced green onions
- 1 tablespoon sesame seeds, toasted

Cook fresh salmon the day it's caught or within 24 hours of purchase. To help maintain its freshness, wrap salmon in plastic wrap or place it in a zip-top plastic bag and refrigerate until time to grill. Leave the skin on the salmon while you grill it. The skin protects the flesh from the heat, so there's no need to turn the fish. Remove and discard the skin before serving.

**1.** To prepare spice mixture, combine first 5 ingredients in a small bowl.

**2.** To prepare glaze, combine rind strips and next 8 ingredients in a saucepan. Bring to a boil. Reduce heat, and simmer 10 minutes. Strain through a sieve; discard solids.

**3.** Prepare grill.

**4.** Rub fillets with spice mixture. Cover; refrigerate 10 minutes. Place fillets, skin sides down, on a grill rack coated with cooking spray. Cover and grill 16 minutes or until fish flakes easily when tested with a fork, basting occasionally with glaze. Remove skin; discard. Arrange fillets on a platter; sprinkle with sliced onions and sesame seeds. Yield: 8 servings (serving size: 1 fillet).

CALORIES 357 (39% from fat); FAT 15.5g (sat 2.7g, mono 7.3g, poly 3.7g); PROTEIN 36.1g; CARB 17g; FIBER 0.3g; CHOL 111mg; IRON 1.5mg; SODIUM 716mg; CALC 32mg

*Salmon is an excellent source of omega-3 oil and vitamins A and B, which may help reduce the risk of heart disease—so eat up! This particular recipe is perfect over a bed of white rice and rounded out with sweet steamed snow peas.*

# Grilled Striped Bass with Chunky Mango-Ginger Sauce

Grilled recipes often call for basting, so a good basting brush is important. The newest brushes are made of dishwasher-safe silicone, but because they don't hold as much liquid as natural bristles, you may need to dip more frequently in the basting liquid.

4 (6-ounce) striped bass or other firm white fish fillets (such as amberjack or grouper)
1 tablespoon olive oil
½ teaspoon kosher salt
¼ teaspoon black pepper
1 cup Chunky Mango-Ginger Sauce

**1.** Prepare grill.
**2.** Brush fillets with oil; sprinkle with salt and pepper. Grill fillets 4 minutes on each side or until fish flakes easily when tested with a fork. Serve with Chunky Mango-Ginger Sauce. Yield: 4 servings (serving size: 1 fillet and ¼ cup sauce).

(Totals include Chunky Mango-Ginger Sauce) CALORIES 296 (34% from fat); FAT 11.3g (sat 2.2g, mono 6.1g, poly 2.1g); PROTEIN 32.9g; CARB 15.3g; FIBER 1.2g; CHOL 116mg; IRON 3mg; SODIUM 363mg; CALC 157mg

## Chunky Mango-Ginger Sauce

1 tablespoon olive oil
2 cups finely chopped red onion
2 cups cubed peeled ripe mango
1 cup chopped tomato
3 tablespoons minced peeled fresh ginger
2 tablespoons minced garlic (about 6 cloves)
½ cup fresh lime juice (about 2 limes)
¼ cup orange juice
¼ cup dry sherry
3 tablespoons brown sugar
3 tablespoons white vinegar

**1.** Heat oil in a large nonstick skillet over medium-high heat. Add onion; sauté 7 minutes. Add mango, tomato, ginger, and garlic; cook 5 minutes. Stir in remaining ingredients; bring to a boil. Reduce heat; simmer 20 minutes, stirring occasionally. Yield: 2½ cups (serving size: ¼ cup).

CALORIES 92 (18% from fat); FAT 1.8g (sat 0.2g, mono 1g, poly 0.2g); PROTEIN 0.8g; CARB 18.5g; FIBER 1.4g; CHOL 0mg; IRON 0.3mg; SODIUM 8mg; CALC 19mg

*Tasty, easy, and beautiful—with just the right combination of savory and sweet—this sauce also makes a great salsa for turkey, chicken, or other mild fish. To make the sauce even chunkier, reduce the final cooking time to 10 minutes.*

# Grilled Tuna over Lemon-Mint Barley Salad

If you're new to grilling fish, fresh tuna is a good starter. It cooks like a beefsteak, and almost never sticks to the grill. Grilling caramelizes the outside and leaves the interior moist. However, since tuna cooks quickly, it needs your constant attention; when overcooked, it can be dry and tough. Many chefs think tuna is best seared on the outside and left almost raw on the inside.

¾ cup finely chopped fresh mint, divided
1 teaspoon grated lemon rind
3 tablespoons plus 1 teaspoon fresh lemon juice, divided
¾ teaspoon salt, divided
½ teaspoon crushed red pepper
3 garlic cloves, minced
4 (6-ounce) Yellowfin tuna steaks
2¼ cups water
1 cup uncooked pearl barley
2 cups chopped tomato
¾ cup chopped green onions
2 tablespoons capers
2 tablespoons chopped pitted kalamata olives
1 tablespoon extravirgin olive oil
Cooking spray

**1.** Combine ½ cup mint, lemon rind, 4 teaspoons lemon juice, ¼ teaspoon salt, pepper, and garlic in a shallow dish; add tuna, turning to coat. Cover and refrigerate 30 minutes.
**2.** While tuna marinates, combine ¼ teaspoon salt and water in a medium saucepan; bring to a boil. Stir in barley; cover, reduce heat, and simmer 30 minutes or until liquid is absorbed. Remove from heat; cover and let stand 5 minutes. Spoon barley into a large bowl; cool slightly. Add remaining ¼ cup mint, tomato, green onions, capers, and olives; stir well to combine. Combine remaining ¼ teaspoon salt, remaining 2 tablespoons lemon juice, and oil, stirring well with a whisk. Drizzle over barley mixture; toss gently to coat.
**3.** Prepare grill.
**4.** Place tuna steaks on a grill rack coated with cooking spray; cook 2 minutes on each side until tuna steaks are medium-rare or desired degree of doneness. Spoon about 1½ cups barley mixture onto each of 4 plates; top each serving with 1 tuna steak. Yield: 4 servings.

CALORIES 415 (15% from fat); FAT 6.9g (sat 1.2g, mono 3.3g, poly 1.6g); PROTEIN 47.2g; CARB 41.9g; FIBER 10.4g; CHOL 77mg; IRON 4mg; SODIUM 685mg; CALC 88mg

*The flavors of the vinaigrette are mirrored in the marinade, so there's a double dose of the refreshing combination of lemon and mint. The salad can be made an hour ahead. You can halve it for two people.*

# Grilled Tuna Sandwiches with Onions, Bell Peppers, and Chile-Cilantro Mayonnaise

Red bell peppers are a good source of the antioxidant beta-carotene, and the amount of bell peppers in just one sandwich delivers almost a whole day's requirement for vitamin C. When buying red bell peppers, make sure they're free of soft spots and wrinkles, which are signs of aging, and their stems are firm and green. "Weigh" a pepper in your hand; it should feel heavy for its size—a sign of thick, juicy flesh. When preparing a bell pepper, cut it in half lengthwise. Using your fingers, scoop out the seeds and membranes, and discard. Grilling the peppers concentrates their flavors.

6 tablespoons light mayonnaise
2 tablespoons chopped fresh cilantro
1 teaspoon ground ancho chile pepper
1 teaspoon grated lime rind
1 teaspoon fresh lime juice
¼ teaspoon ground chipotle chile pepper
5 teaspoons olive oil, divided
4 (¼-inch-thick) slices sweet onion
1 red bell pepper, seeded and quartered
½ teaspoon salt, divided
4 (5-ounce) tuna steaks (about ¾ inch thick)
¼ teaspoon ground cumin
¼ teaspoon freshly ground black pepper
4 (2-ounce) sandwich buns
4 red leaf lettuce leaves

**1.** Heat a grill pan over medium-high heat.
**2.** Combine first 6 ingredients in a small bowl.
**3.** Brush 3 teaspoons oil evenly over onion and bell pepper; sprinkle with ¼ teaspoon salt. Place onion and bell pepper on grill pan; cook 3½ minutes on each side or until tender. Remove from pan; keep warm.
**4.** Brush 2 teaspoons oil evenly over tuna; sprinkle with ¼ teaspoon salt, cumin, and black pepper. Place tuna on grill pan; cook 3½ minutes on each side or until medium-rare or desired degree of doneness.
**5.** Split buns in half horizontally. Spread mayonnaise mixture evenly over cut sides of buns. Top bottom half of each bun with 1 lettuce leaf, 1 bell pepper quarter, 1 onion slice, and 1 tuna steak. Cover with top halves of buns. Yield: 4 servings (serving size: 1 sandwich).

CALORIES 452 (35% from fat); FAT 17.5g (sat 3.2g, mono 5.1g, poly 2.3g); PROTEIN 37.1g; CARB 37.2g; FIBER 5.9g; CHOL 74mg; IRON 3.7mg; SODIUM 802mg; CALC 122mg

*The tangy citrus quality of this mayonnaise pairs well with the grilled tuna. Plus, it's extremely versatile—you can use it on different kinds of burgers and sandwiches. This sandwich can be spicy, so reduce the amount of ground chipotle chile pepper if you prefer a milder taste.*

# Zesty Swordfish Kebabs

Fresh swordfish appears in markets year-round, usually as steak, and is generally best when it's grilled or pan-fried. When you're making kebabs, be sure to cut the swordfish into pieces that are roughly the same size to ensure even cooking on the grill. Popular for its mild flavor and meaty texture, swordfish became endangered in the early '90s, and in 1997, conservation groups called on chefs and consumers to boycott it. The swordfish population is slowly recovering with careful management of its fishery.

3 tablespoons low-sodium soy sauce
2 tablespoons chopped fresh rosemary
2 tablespoons fresh lemon juice
1 tablespoon grated lemon rind
1½ tablespoons extravirgin olive oil
2 teaspoons grated orange rind
1 tablespoon fresh orange juice
2 teaspoons honey
1 teaspoon grated peeled fresh ginger
½ teaspoon salt
¼ teaspoon freshly ground black pepper
5 garlic cloves, chopped
1½ pounds swordfish steaks, cut into 1-inch pieces
¾ cup (2-inch) sliced green onions
12 (1-inch) pieces red bell pepper
Cooking spray

**1.** Combine first 12 ingredients in a large zip-top plastic bag; add fish. Seal and marinate in refrigerator 30 minutes, turning once.
**2.** Prepare grill.
**3.** Remove fish from bag; discard marinade. Thread fish, green onions, and bell pepper alternately onto each of 4 (10-inch) skewers. Place skewers on a grill rack coated with cooking spray; grill 8 minutes or until desired degree of doneness, turning once. Yield: 4 servings (serving size: 1 kebab).

CALORIES 248 (28% from fat); FAT 7.8g (sat 2g, mono 3.4g, poly 1.7g); PROTEIN 33.8g; CARB 9.7g; FIBER 1.6g; CHOL 64mg; IRON 2mg; SODIUM 711mg; CALC 38mg

*This recipe is perfect for both family and company. A side of grilled vegetables completes this quick-and-easy meal. Use the marinade for grilled swordfish steaks, too.*

# Grilled Clams with Sambuca and Italian Sausage

There are two main types of clams: soft-shell and hard-shell. Both types vary in size. Generally, the smaller the clam, the more tender the meat. The clams most often sold in markets are hard-shell. To clean clams, scrub them under cold running water with a stiff brush to remove sand and dirt.

4 ounces hot turkey Italian sausage
¼ cup finely chopped onion
¼ cup finely chopped green bell pepper
¼ cup finely chopped red bell pepper
½ teaspoon butter
1 garlic clove, minced
1 (1-ounce) slice day-old white bread
2 tablespoons Sambuca or Pernod (licorice-flavored liqueur)
½ teaspoon Worcestershire sauce
⅛ teaspoon black pepper
Dash of salt
36 littleneck clams, cleaned
6 lemon wedges

**1.** Remove casings from sausage. Heat a large nonstick skillet over medium heat. Add sausage; cook until browned, stirring to crumble. Add onion, bell peppers, butter, and garlic to pan; cook 5 minutes, stirring frequently.
**2.** Place bread in a food processor; pulse 5 times or until breadcrumbs form. Add breadcrumbs to sausage mixture; cook 3 minutes, stirring constantly. Pour Sambuca into one side of skillet. Ignite Sambuca with a long match, and let flames die down. Stir in the Worcestershire sauce, pepper, and salt.
**3.** Prepare grill.
**4.** Shuck clams; discard top halves of shells and any broken shells or shells that remain open. Place 12 clam halves on a shellfish grate. Top each with about 1 teaspoon breadcrumb mixture. Place grate on grill. Cover and cook 4 minutes or until clam juice in shells boils. Remove clams from grate; keep warm. Repeat procedure with remaining clams and breadcrumbs. Serve with lemon wedges. Yield: 6 servings (serving size: 6 clams and 1 lemon wedge).

CALORIES 120 (23% from fat); FAT 3.1g (sat 0.8g, mono 0.8g, poly 0.6g); PROTEIN 15g; CARB 6.2g; FIBER 0.4g; CHOL 44mg; IRON 5.9mg; SODIUM 221mg; CALC 38mg

*A vegetable grill grate can be used in place of a shellfish grate. Or buy bigger clams; you can set them directly on the grill rack. Store clams in an open bowl in the refrigerator, and use them as soon as possible. Don't store clams in a sealed plastic bag or on ice because they'll die.*

# Scallops with Roasted Pepper-Butter Sauce

The double-skewer technique is ideal for grilling scallops, shrimp, or fruits and vegetables that tend to wobble when threaded on one skewer. To double-skewer, just thread the scallops onto a skewer, then run another skewer through the scallops parallel to the first. This technique makes it easier to turn the skewers, too. If using wooden skewers, be sure to soak them in water at least 30 minutes before using them.

30 sea scallops (about 2¼ pounds)
 4 red bell peppers (about 2 pounds)
 2 cups fat-free, less-sodium chicken broth
 ½ cup dry white wine
1½ teaspoons chopped fresh or ½ teaspoon dried basil, crumbled
 2 tablespoons chilled butter, cut into small pieces
 ¼ teaspoon salt
Cooking spray
Basil sprigs (optional)

**1.** Thread 5 scallops onto each of 6 (12-inch) skewers. Cover and chill.
**2.** Preheat broiler.
**3.** Cut peppers in half lengthwise; discard seeds and membranes. Place pepper halves, skin sides up, on a foil-lined baking sheet; flatten with hand. Broil 15 minutes or until blackened. Place in a zip-top plastic bag. Seal and let stand 10 minutes. Peel peppers; discard skins. Place peppers, broth, and wine in a blender; process until smooth. Combine pepper mixture and chopped basil in a skillet. Bring to a boil; cook until reduced to 1½ cups (about 5 minutes). Reduce heat to medium-low; gradually add butter, stirring until melted. Cover and keep warm.
**4.** Prepare grill.
**5.** Sprinkle kabobs with salt; place on a grill rack coated with cooking spray. Grill 2½ minutes on each side or until done. Serve with bell pepper sauce. Garnish with basil, if desired. Yield: 6 servings (serving size: 5 scallops and ¼ cup sauce).

CALORIES 208 (23% from fat); FAT 5.2g (sat 2.5g, mono 1.2g, poly 0.7g); PROTEIN 29.8g; CARB 9.4g; FIBER 1.6g; CHOL 67mg; IRON 0.9mg; SODIUM 970mg; CALC 52mg

*Scallops are usually classified into two groups: bay scallops and sea scallops. The larger sea scallops are best for grilling because, like shrimp, they have a meatier texture and can be easily skewered. They cook fast, so keep a close eye on them.*

# Spicy Grilled Jumbo Shrimp

2¼ pounds unpeeled jumbo
    shrimp
¾ cup Honeyed Lemon-Dijon
    Vinaigrette, divided
½ teaspoon crushed red
    pepper
¼ teaspoon salt
¼ teaspoon coarsely ground
    black pepper
Cooking spray
Lemon wedges

**1.** Peel shrimp, leaving tails intact. Starting at tail end, butterfly each shrimp, cutting to, but not through, underside of shrimp. Combine shrimp, 6 tablespoons Honeyed Lemon-Dijon Vinaigrette, and red pepper in a large zip-top plastic bag. Seal bag, and marinate in refrigerator 15 minutes, turning bag occasionally.
**2.** Prepare grill.
**3.** Remove shrimp from marinade; discard marinade. Sprinkle shrimp with salt and black pepper. Place, cut sides down, on a grill rack coated with cooking spray; grill 2 minutes on each side, basting frequently with 6 tablespoons Honeyed Lemon-Dijon Vinaigrette. Serve with lemon wedges. Yield: 6 servings (serving size: about 4½ ounces).

(Totals include Honeyed Lemon-Dijon Vinaigrette) CALORIES 223 (27% from fat); FAT 6.6g (sat 1.1g, mono 3.2g, poly 1.5g); PROTEIN 34.7g; CARB 4.1g; FIBER 0.3g; CHOL 259mg; IRON 4.2mg; SODIUM 549mg; CALC 93mg

It's important to use butterflied jumbo shrimp for this recipe. Otherwise, the shrimp will be too small and may fall through the grill rack. To butterfly shrimp, split the shrimp down the center of the back of the shrimp using a sharp knife, cutting almost through the shrimp. Open the halves flat, making a butterfly shape. Butterflying the shrimp gives it an attractive appearance and more surface area for the marinade to penetrate.

## Honeyed Lemon-Dijon Vinaigrette

¼ cup chopped fresh dill
¼ cup white wine vinegar
2 tablespoons chopped red
    onion
2 tablespoons capers
1 tablespoon grated lemon rind
2 tablespoons fresh lemon juice
4 teaspoons honey
2 teaspoons Dijon mustard
1 teaspoon salt
¾ teaspoon freshly ground
    black pepper
½ teaspoon hot pepper sauce
2 garlic cloves, minced
⅓ cup boiling water
¼ cup extravirgin olive oil

**1.** Place first 12 ingredients in a blender; process until mixture is smooth. Add water and oil; process until well combined. Yield: about 1½ cups (serving size: 1 tablespoon).
**Note:** Refrigerate vinaigrette in an airtight container up to five days, and stir well before using.

CALORIES 27 (80% from fat); FAT 2.4g (sat 0.3g, mono 1.8g, poly 0.2g); PROTEIN 0.1g; CARB 1.6g; FIBER 0.1g; CHOL 0mg; IRON 0.1mg; SODIUM 133mg; CALC 2mg

*This easy entrée is great for casual backyard get-togethers. Make the vinaigrette ahead; then the recipe takes less than 30 minutes to prepare. This dish has a light, citrusy, summertime taste, yet gets an extra jolt of flavor from the hot red pepper sauce.*

# Shrimp on Sugarcane with Rum Glaze

Look for sugarcane swizzle sticks in the produce section, or order them from www.melissas.com. If you can't find sugarcane, bamboo skewers will do in a pinch.

1 tablespoon canola oil
1 tablespoon fresh lemon juice
¼ teaspoon black pepper
⅛ teaspoon salt
1 garlic clove, minced
24 jumbo shrimp, peeled and deveined (about 1½ pounds)
8 sugarcane swizzle sticks, each cut into 3 pieces
¼ cup packed dark brown sugar
¼ cup dark rum
¼ cup corn syrup
3 tablespoons Dijon mustard
1 tablespoon white vinegar
1 tablespoon butter
¼ teaspoon salt
¼ teaspoon ground cinnamon
¼ teaspoon black pepper
Cooking spray

**1.** Prepare grill.
**2.** Combine first 5 ingredients in a large bowl. Add shrimp; toss to coat. Cover and chill 15 minutes.
**3.** Cut ends of swizzle sticks at a sharp angle. Thread 1 shrimp on each skewer.
**4.** Combine brown sugar and next 8 ingredients in a saucepan, and bring to a boil. Reduce heat, and simmer 5 minutes or until syrupy.
**5.** Place shrimp skewers on a grill rack coated with cooking spray. Grill 3 minutes on each side or until done, basting generously with glaze. Yield: 6 servings (serving size: 4 shrimp).

CALORIES 217 (22% from fat); FAT 5.2g (sat 1.6g, mono 2g, poly 1.1g); PROTEIN 18.1g; CARB 22.1g; FIBER 0.1g; CHOL 173mg; IRON 3mg; SODIUM 464mg; CALC 48mg

*Caribbean-influenced shrimp, skewered with sugarcane and basted with a dark rum glaze, rely on high heat to caramelize the glaze and infuse the shrimp from the inside out with the cane's mild sweetness.*

# fruits & vegetables

# Grilled Asparagus Rafts

16 thick asparagus spears
   (about 1 pound)
 1 tablespoon low-sodium soy
   sauce
 1 teaspoon dark sesame oil
 1 garlic clove, minced
 2 teaspoons sesame seeds,
   toasted
¼ teaspoon black pepper
Dash of salt

**1.** Prepare grill.
**2.** Snap off tough ends of asparagus. Arrange 4 asparagus spears on a flat surface. Thread 2 (3-inch) skewers or wooden picks horizontally through spears 1 inch from each end to form a raft. Repeat procedure with remaining asparagus spears.
**3.** Combine soy sauce, oil, and garlic; brush evenly over asparagus rafts. Grill 3 minutes on each side or until crisp-tender. Sprinkle evenly with sesame seeds, pepper, and salt. Yield: 4 servings (serving size: 1 asparagus raft).

CALORIES 50 (38% from fat); FAT 2.1g (sat 0.2g, mono 0.5g, poly 0.6g); PROTEIN 3.2g; CARB 6.1g; FIBER 2.4g; CHOL 0mg; IRON 3mg; SODIUM 190mg; CALC 26mg

Choose asparagus spears with tight, compact tips and a similar diameter so they'll all cook at the same rate. To snap off the tough ends, hold both ends of each spear and bend; the tough, fibrous base should snap right off. (This step is unnecessary in thinner spears, which are completely edible.)

*This recipe is a nice twist on traditional grilled asparagus spears. Skewering groups of asparagus spears together makes them easier to flip on the grill. Sesame seeds lend additional crunch and a sprinkling of color to the dark green spears. The secret for cooking asparagus is simple: don't overcook it. The slender shoots should turn out crisp and bright in color.*

# Grilled Eggplant with Caramelized Onion and Fennel

Extremely versatile, eggplant responds to a variety of cooking methods. Dry heat, such as grilling and broiling, concentrates flavor and transforms the texture to a tender, almost creamy consistency. First, peel the eggplant, then, cut it into pieces that are the same thickness to ensure even cooking.

1 (1¼-pound) eggplant (about 4-inch diameter), peeled
Cooking spray
¼ teaspoon salt, divided
¼ teaspoon freshly ground black pepper, divided
2¾ cups chopped fennel bulb (about 1 large bulb)
2 cups finely chopped yellow onion
2 cups trimmed arugula
1 teaspoon white balsamic vinegar
1 teaspoon extravirgin olive oil
1 cup quartered cherry tomatoes
½ cup (2 ounces) crumbled goat cheese
2 tablespoons chopped fresh basil
1 tablespoon chopped fresh thyme

**1.** Prepare grill.

**2.** Cut peeled eggplant crosswise into 8 (½-inch-thick) slices. Lightly coat both sides of slices with cooking spray; sprinkle with ⅛ teaspoon salt and ⅛ teaspoon pepper. Place on a grill rack coated with cooking spray; grill 7 minutes on each side or until browned. Set eggplant slices aside.

**3.** Heat a large nonstick skillet over medium-high heat. Coat pan with cooking spray. Add fennel and onion; sauté 8 minutes or until vegetables are tender and lightly browned.

**4.** Combine ⅛ teaspoon salt, ⅛ teaspoon pepper, arugula, vinegar, and oil in a medium bowl; toss gently to coat. Divide arugula mixture evenly among 8 appetizer plates; top each serving with 1 eggplant slice. Arrange about ⅓ cup fennel mixture on each eggplant slice; top with 2 tablespoons tomatoes and 1 tablespoon cheese. Sprinkle basil and thyme evenly over cheese. Yield: 8 servings.

CALORIES 73 (30% from fat); FAT 2.4g (sat 1.2g, mono 0.8g, poly 0.2g); PROTEIN 3.2g; CARB 11.3g; FIBER 3.8g; CHOL 3mg; IRON 0.9mg; SODIUM 122mg; CALC 49mg

*To prepare this appetizer indoors, broil the eggplant rounds until browned, and continue the recipe as instructed. White balsamic vinegar offers the sweetness of regular balsamic but won't discolor the salad. You can use regular balsamic vinegar if white isn't available.*

# Portobello Burgers

Portobello mushroom caps, with their meaty texture and intense flavor, are great for grilling. They often measure from 3 to 6 inches across so they don't fall through the grill rack. They are a perfect fit for a round sandwich bun, too. The portobello stands up to bold flavors such as acidic marinades, fresh rosemary and basil, and chile peppers.

¼ cup low-sodium soy sauce
¼ cup balsamic vinegar
2 tablespoons olive oil
3 garlic cloves, minced
4 (4-inch) portobello
   mushroom caps
1 small red bell pepper
Cooking spray
¼ cup low-fat mayonnaise
½ teaspoon olive oil
⅛ teaspoon ground red
   pepper
4 (2-ounce) onion sandwich
   buns
4 (¼-inch-thick) slices tomato
4 curly leaf lettuce leaves

**1.** Combine first 4 ingredients in a large zip-top plastic bag; add mushrooms to bag. Seal and marinate at room temperature 2 hours, turning bag occasionally. Remove mushrooms from bag; discard marinade.
**2.** Prepare grill.
**3.** Cut bell pepper in half lengthwise; discard seeds and membranes. Place pepper halves on a grill rack coated with cooking spray; grill 15 minutes or until blackened, turning occasionally. Place in a zip-top plastic bag; seal. Let stand 10 minutes. Peel. Reserve 1 pepper half for another use. Finely chop 1 pepper half; place in a small bowl. Add mayonnaise, ½ teaspoon oil, and ground red pepper; stir well.
**4.** Place mushrooms, gill sides down, on grill rack coated with cooking spray; grill 4 minutes on each side. Place buns, cut sides down, on grill rack coated with cooking spray; grill 30 seconds on each side or until toasted. Spread 2 tablespoons mayonnaise mixture on top half of each bun. Place 1 mushroom on bottom half of each bun. Top each mushroom with 1 tomato slice and 1 lettuce leaf; cover with top halves of buns. Yield: 4 servings (serving size: 1 burger).

CALORIES 285 (38% from fat); FAT 11.6g (sat 2.6g, mono 2.9g, poly 0.5g); PROTEIN 9g; CARB 34.7g; FIBER 2.6g; CHOL 5mg; IRON 1.9mg; SODIUM 699mg; CALC 78mg

*Because of the portobello's firm texture, these burgers will please both vegetarians and nonvegetarians alike. Half of a roasted bell pepper is stirred into mayonnaise for the sandwich spread. Use the leftover bell pepper as a pizza topping, or in a salad or a pasta dish.*

# Grilled Fries

2 teaspoons paprika
1 teaspoon sea or kosher salt
1 teaspoon coarsely ground black pepper
½ teaspoon garlic powder
½ teaspoon onion powder
½ teaspoon chili powder
1 teaspoon olive oil
2 baking potatoes, each cut into 12 wedges (about 1½ pounds)
2 sweet potatoes, each cut into 12 wedges (about 1½ pounds)
Cooking spray

**1.** Combine first 6 ingredients. Combine oil and potatoes in a large bowl, tossing to coat. Sprinkle potatoes with paprika mixture; toss gently to coat.
**2.** Prepare grill.
**3.** Place potatoes on a grill rack coated with cooking spray over medium heat; grill 18 minutes or until sweet potatoes are tender, turning occasionally. Remove sweet potatoes; keep warm. Grill baking potatoes an additional 6 minutes or until tender. Yield: 6 servings (serving size: 8 fries).

CALORIES 171 (5% from fat); FAT 1g (sat 0.2g, mono 0.6g, poly 0.2g); PROTEIN 3.9g; CARB 37.9g; FIBER 4.3g; CHOL 0mg; IRON 1.7mg; SODIUM 441mg; CALC 43mg

Potatoes and sweet potatoes aren't in the same family, despite the notion that two things that look alike must be related. Baking potatoes are long, dusky brown tubers with numerous eyes, and are starchy, floury, large, and slightly nutty. Idaho produces almost a third of the country's potato crop. Sweet potatoes, on the other hand, are warm-weather plants, happy in the Caribbean and other hot, humid climates. The contrasting flavors of starchy and sweet provide a unique, tasty twist in this recipe. There's no need to peel these potatoes before cutting them into wedges and grilling.

*Serve these fries with Grilled Porterhouse Steak (recipe on page 40). If you have a large enough grill, start grilling the potatoes with the steak so everything will be done at the same time. Otherwise, tent the beef with foil to keep it warm. This perfect combination will guarantee rave reviews from friends and family.*

# Tandoori Tofu and Vegetable Kebabs

Normally, tofu is soft and crumbly. Threading cubes of it on skewers would be impossible. However, prebaking the tofu toughens the proteins and pulls out excess water. The baked tofu has a texture similar to firm fish, making it easier to handle while skewering and grilling.

1 (16-ounce) package water-packed firm tofu, drained and cut into 16 cubes
Cooking spray
1 cup finely chopped onion
¾ cup plain low-fat yogurt
2 teaspoons grated peeled fresh ginger
2 teaspoons canola oil
2 teaspoons ground coriander
1½ teaspoons ground cumin
½ teaspoon ground turmeric
¼ teaspoon freshly ground black pepper
1 garlic clove, minced
16 large mushrooms (about 10 ounces)
2 small red onions, each cut into 8 wedges
2⅔ cups water
1⅓ cups uncooked basmati rice
⅔ cup golden raisins
1 teaspoon salt, divided

**1.** Preheat oven to 375°.
**2.** Arrange tofu in a single layer on a foil-lined baking sheet coated with cooking spray. Bake at 375° for 25 minutes or until tofu releases 3 or more tablespoons liquid.
**3.** Combine chopped onion and next 8 ingredients in a large bowl. Add tofu, mushrooms, and onion wedges; toss gently to coat. Let stand at room temperature 30 minutes.
**4.** While tofu and vegetables marinate, prepare rice. Bring water to a boil in a medium saucepan; stir in rice. Cover, reduce heat, and simmer 15 minutes or until liquid is absorbed. Stir in raisins and ¼ teaspoon salt. Let stand 5 minutes; fluff with a fork.
**5.** Prepare grill.
**6.** Remove tofu and vegetables from bowl; discard marinade. Thread tofu cubes, mushrooms, and onion wedges alternately onto 8 (6-inch) skewers. Lightly coat kebabs with cooking spray; sprinkle with ¾ teaspoon salt. Place kebabs on a grill rack coated with cooking spray; grill 4 minutes on each side or until lightly browned. Serve kebabs with rice. Yield: 4 servings (serving size: 2 kebabs and 1 cup rice).

CALORIES 421 (21% from fat); FAT 9.6g (sat 1.7g, mono 1.9g, poly 5g); PROTEIN 20.2g; CARB 72.9g; FIBER 5.4g; CHOL 2mg; IRON 4.9mg; SODIUM 625mg; CALC 190mg

*Golden raisins in the rice pilaf are a sweet balance to the intense spices in the tandoori marinade. Both tofu's subtle flavor and tender texture merge well with a multitude of Western and Asian seasonings. The variety of flavors in this dish makes it a healthy, instant classic.*

# Marinated Grilled Apples with Mint

⅔ cup fresh orange juice
1 tablespoon chopped fresh mint
2 tablespoons honey
1 teaspoon vanilla extract
½ teaspoon ground ginger
¼ teaspoon black pepper
3 Granny Smith apples, cored and each cut crosswise into 4 (½-inch) slices
Cooking spray

**1.** Combine first 6 ingredients in a large zip-top plastic bag. Add apple slices; seal and marinate in refrigerator 1 to 2 hours, turning bag occasionally.
**2.** Prepare grill.
**3.** Remove apple from bag, reserving marinade. Place apple slices on a grill rack coated with cooking spray; grill 3 minutes on each side, turning and basting frequently with reserved marinade. Arrange apple slices on a platter; drizzle with any remaining marinade. Yield: 4 servings (serving size: 3 apple slices).

CALORIES 116 (4% from fat); FAT 0.5g (sat 0.1g, mono 0g, poly 0.1g); PROTEIN 0.6g; CARB 29.3g; FIBER 3g; CHOL 0mg; IRON 0.4mg; SODIUM 1mg; CALC 14mg

Granny Smith is a hard, crunchy, green-skinned apple with a tart, crisp flavor. It's a juicy apple that keeps its flavor well, making it ideal for grilling. There's no need to peel the apples, but be sure to cut them into even, thick slices.

*Serve these highly flavored apple rings as a side with pork or chicken. (One serving size for this recipe is three apple slices, but you can easily double the number of slices for even larger, guilt-free portions of this healthy dish.) We liked this recipe with Granny Smiths. For a dessert version, use Pink Lady apples, and serve with low-fat ice cream.*

# Grilled Plantains

3 soft black plantains,
    unpeeled (about 1½
    pounds)
2 tablespoons butter, melted
1 teaspoon brown sugar
⅛ teaspoon ground red
    pepper
Cooking spray
6 lime wedges

**1.** Prepare grill, heating to medium.
**2.** Cut plantains in half lengthwise. Cut plantain halves in half crosswise. Combine butter, sugar, and pepper; brush evenly over cut sides of plantain sections.
**3.** Place plantain sections, cut sides up, on a grill rack coated with cooking spray; grill 7 minutes or until flesh is soft and skins begin to pull away from flesh. Turn plantain sections over; grill 3 minutes. Serve warm with lime wedges. Yield: 6 servings (serving size: 2 plantain sections and 1 lime wedge).

CALORIES 174 (22% from fat); FAT 4.3g (sat 2.6g, mono 1.2g, poly 0.2g); PROTEIN 1.5g; CARB 36.7g; FIBER 2.6g; CHOL 10mg; IRON 0.7mg; SODIUM 44mg; CALC 5mg

Plantains, pronounced PLAN-tihns, usually have less sugar and are firmer than common, sweet bananas. Although immature green-skinned plantains are used in many Latin American dishes, ripe plantains are necessary here. More than likely you'll find plantains in your supermarket that are just beginning to turn black. Go ahead and purchase these. Just let them sit at room temperature for a few days until they turn black and feel soft when lightly pressed. Black plantains are extremely ripe, and their deep yellow pulp is much sweeter than green plantains. You can eat a very ripe plantain raw.

*Because the ripe plantains are so tender, they're grilled in their skins to keep them in one piece. Try with Rum-Marinated Chicken Breasts with Pineapple Relish (recipe on page 76). A ripe plantain is believed to be more easily digestible than a ripe banana and is widely known for its health benefits. Also, be careful if you want to try to peel a plantain, since the juice can stain clothing and skin, and is very difficult to remove.*

# Rum-Spiked Grilled Pineapple

1 pineapple, peeled, cored,
halved lengthwise, and
sliced lengthwise into 12
wedges (about 1½ pounds)
2 tablespoons butter, melted
¼ cup packed light brown
sugar
¼ cup dark rum
¼ teaspoon ground cinnamon
Cooking spray
Flaked sweetened coconut,
toasted (optional)
Vanilla light ice cream (optional)

**1.** Prepare grill.
**2.** Brush pineapple wedges with 2 tablespoons butter. Combine brown sugar, rum and ¼ teaspoon cinnamon in a microwave-safe bowl. Microwave at HIGH 1½ minutes or until sugar dissolves. Brush rum mixture evenly over pineapple wedges. Place pineapple on a grill rack coated with cooking spray. Grill 3 minutes on each side or until grill marks form and pineapple is thoroughly heated. Top with toasted coconut and serve with ice cream, if desired. Yield: 6 servings (serving size: 2 pineapple wedges).

CALORIES 146 (25% from fat); FAT 4g (sat 2.4g, mono 1g, poly 0.2g); PROTEIN 0.7g; CARB 23.4g; FIBER 1.6g; CHOL 10mg; IRON 0.5mg; SODIUM 32mg; CALC 25mg

Pineapples can be easy to peel and core as long as you know the technique. Cut about 1 inch from each end. Stand the pineapple vertically on the cutting board. Slice down about ½ inch into the skin. This should remove the eyes from the pineapple flesh. Keep turning the pineapple with one hand and slicing 1-inch-wide bands down in a straight line until the pine-apple is peeled. Then, cut the fruit into quarters. While hold-ing each pineapple quarter firmly, remove the core. Cut the pineapple wedges in half lengthwise, then cut as need-ed for this recipe.

*Grilling caramelizes the natural sugars in the fresh pineapple. Serve as a side dish with barbecued chicken or pork for summer cookouts. Add a scoop of vanilla light ice cream and a sprinkling of toasted coconut to transform the grilled pineapple spears into a dessert that not only looks gorgeous, but is also a sweet and healthy finale for your guests.*

# all about
# Grilling

Be it a burger, a steak, or a veggie, grill like a pro with this Cooking Class as your guide. Master these tips and techniques, and you'll be the next backyard barbecue extraordinaire.

## Grilling Basics

**Quality Ingredients.** Always start with quality ingredients. Because it's a dry, high-heat cooking method, grilling accentuates the natural flavor of food. No amount of seasoning will change the essential quality of the ingredients you use, so start with the best cuts of meat, poultry, seafood, and the freshest fruits and vegetables.

**Charcoal or Gas?** Our staff doesn't really have a preference for one type of grilling over the other. Some people claim to detect a taste advantage with charcoal, but we really haven't found that to be the case as long as the two fuels provide a similar temperature range. We've cooked on several good gas grills, and the results are always just as tasty as those from charcoal.

**Fast (Direct):** Direct grilling involves putting food on a grill rack directly over hot coals. The best candidates for direct grilling are firm-fleshed fish and shellfish such as salmon, tuna, swordfish, halibut, mahimahi, and shrimp; chicken breasts and thighs; chops; burgers; and steaks. Vegetables can also be grilled directly—just be sure to cut them large enough so that they don't fall through the rack, or use a grill basket.

**Slow (Indirect):** This method is similar to oven-roasting. Both sides of the grill are fired up, then one side is turned off. If using a charcoal grill, push the hot coals to one side. A disposable aluminum foil pan (also called a drip pan) containing water (or wine, broth, or other liquid) is placed directly over the coals on the side of a gas or electric grill where the heat has been turned off. On a charcoal grill, the pan is placed on the side where the charcoal has been moved. The food is then placed on the rack over the pan. The pan serves two purposes: It creates a steamy environment in which the food can cook, and it catches drippings from the food, minimizing flare-ups. Good candidates for this type of grilling include whole chickens, roasts, turkey breasts, and other large foods. To further intensify flavor, brown food over direct heat at the start or end of grilling.

**Covered or Uncovered?**
As a rule, cover the grill when grilling large pieces of food using the indirect method. Resist the temptation to peek; you lose all the built-up heat and add 5 to 10 minutes to your cook time for each peek. Leave the grill uncovered when doing fast or direct grilling with smaller items that cook quickly.

135

# The Right Fire for the Food

When grilling, choosing the right level of heat for the food is crucial.
Here are the temperatures that work best with particular foods.

## Medium Heat
- Bell peppers, corn on the cob (shucked), eggplant, and most other vegetables
- Chicken breasts and halves
- Duck breasts
- Pork chops and most other pork cuts
- Pork ribs (after baking in an oven or cooking on a covered grill until tender)
- Turkey fillets
- Veal chops (can also cook on medium-low)

## Medium-High Heat
- Most fish and shellfish

## High Heat
- Calamari
- Salmon fillets and steaks
- Scallops
- Shrimp (peeled)

## Sear on high heat; finish on medium
- Beef steaks
- Pork tenderloin
- Chicken thighs and drumsticks
- Hamburgers (switch to medium after searing each side 1 minute)
- Lamb chops and butterflied leg of lamb
- Tuna steaks
- Uncooked sausage
- Venison steaks

**How Hot?**

The best way to measure the temperature of an open fire is the time-honored hand test. Simply hold your hand about 3 inches above the grate, then time how long you can keep your hand there before you're forced to withdraw it.

- 1 to 2 seconds—signifies a hot fire that's perfect for searing a steak or grilling shrimp
- 3 seconds—indicates medium-high heat, which is great for most fish
- 4 to 5 seconds—signifies a medium range, ideal for most chicken and vegetables
- 7 to 8 seconds—indicates the temperature is low and perfect for grilling delicate vegetables and fruit

## Thermometer Readings

To prevent foodborne illnesses, you'll want to use an instant-read thermometer to gauge doneness. Insert the thermometer into the center of the thickest part of the food and away from the bone. The following is a list of safe temperatures for particular foods:

- Beef: at least 145°
- Pork: at least 160°
- Lamb: at least 145°
- Poultry: at least 165°

Thermometers that come with most grills measure only temperatures inside the grill when the cover is closed. If you cook with direct heat with the cover down, you get a measurement of the reflected heat that contributes to the cooking process, but you don't get the actual grilling temperature on the grate where the food sits. The top side of the food is cooked at the oven temperature indicated, while the bottom side directly above the fire is grilled at a higher temperature.

## Meat Safety

Because you're working close to the heat source and dealing with an outside temperature, safety is always an issue when you're grilling. Here are our safety "musts."

- Marinate food in the refrigerator, not on the countertop.
- Never desert your post. Pay attention. Even though grilling is easy, it requires vigilance because of flame-ups and other potential problems.
- Any contamination in the raw meat can be transferred from the meat to the marinade. If you use the marinade as a basting sauce, or serve it alongside the grilled food, you must place the marinade in a small saucepan, bring it to a boil, and boil for 1 minute to kill any germs that might have been transferred from the food.
- Use an instant-read thermometer (as suggested at left).
- Place grilled foods on a clean platter or cutting board.

## Stovetop Grill Pan

A grill pan is also another cooking option when grilling—especially if it's cold or rainy outside. And a grill pan adds more than just pretty grill marks and smoky flavors. Its ridges elevate food so air can circulate underneath and fat can drip away, so your food doesn't sauté or steam as it does in a plain skillet; instead, flavor is seared into the food. Meat and fish turn out juicy, with no need for added fat. Vegetables stay crisp-tender, and their nutrients don't leach out into cooking water.

## Buying a Stovetop Grill Pan

You can buy grill pans at your local discount or kitchen store for less than $20 to more than $100; nonstick pans are also available. Here are some things to look for.

- High ridges produce results similar to those of an outdoor grill. If the ridges are too low, you might as well be using a regular skillet.
- Low sides make flipping burgers and removing food with a spatula much easier.
- A pan with a square or oblong shape holds more food than a round pan.
- A lidless pan is a good choice, since there's no reason to lock in moisture when grilling.
- Nonstick grill pans are easier to clean than cast-iron pans.
- There's no specific brand that we think is better, but we do prefer to use the larger-sized pans.

# Essential Secrets for Grilling Success

Here are our top 10 secrets for grilling perfection.

**1. Be organized.** Have the food, marinade, sauces, and utensils grillside and ready to go before you start cooking. Make sure you have enough gas or charcoal before you start.

**2. Take the chill off.** Take marinated meats out of the refrigerator and let them stand at room temperature for 10 to 15 minutes before grilling, so you won't end up with a cold center.

**3. Keep it clean.** We recommend cleaning your grill twice: once after preheating the grill, and again when you've finished grilling. Use both a metal spatula and a wire brush to scrape the grates clean.

**4. Coat the grate with cooking spray** or oil before placing food on it. This seasons the grill, helps clean it, and helps prevent food from sticking. If using oil, quickly run a paper towel that is moist with oil over the grates.

**5. Know when to baste.** Many people ruin great food by basting it too early with sugar-based sauces, which results in charring. To prevent burning, add sugar-based sauces toward the end of the cook time. You can baste with yogurt-, citrus-, or oil and vinegar–based sauces throughout cooking. If you use the marinade to baste, stop just before the last 3 minutes of cooking.

**6. Go light on the sugar** in homemade sauces, and avoid those bottled sauces that are mostly sugar and salt. Sometimes all you need to add flavor to grilled food is a little salt and pepper.

**7. Give it a rest.** Meat will taste better and be juicier if given a chance to rest a few minutes after you take it off the grill.

**8. Turn; don't stab.** Use tongs or a spatula to turn the meat but avoid the urge to press on the meat with the

spatula. Don't use a carving fork because it pierces the food and lets out flavorful juices.

**9. Don't overcook.** Know in advance how long you expect to grill the food, and set a timer to alert you to check it. For large cuts of meat and poultry, use an instant-read meat thermometer to gauge doneness.

**10. Control flare-ups,** and don't let food burn. Avoid charring meat and don't eat any part that is especially burned and black. Cooking meats at high temperatures creates chemicals that may increase the risk of cancer. When dripping fat produces a flame in one spot, move food to a different area on the grill. Keep a spray bottle of water by the grill to put out accidental flare-ups. Also, you're less likely to have flames when you keep the oil in the marinade to a minimum.

# Essential Techniques for Grilling Meat

At Cooking Light we've figured out what it takes to grill great steaks. Here are some helpful hints that will ensure you get the results you're looking for every time you throw a steak on the grill.

## Mark Matters

For an attractive presentation, grill crosshatches on steak.

**1.** Set steak on grill.

**2.** After about a minute—or halfway through the cooking time for the first side of the steak—rotate the meat a quarter-turn (45° for diamond-shaped crosshatches, 90° for square-shaped marks).

**3.** Flip steak over, and complete cooking. Only one side of the steak will show on the plate, so both sides don't require crosshatches. Do not flip steak back onto marked side while grilling.

## Degrees of Doneness

While doneness standards can vary somewhat (one person's rare may be another's medium-rare), we follow U.S. Department of Agriculture guidelines for steak temperatures. The USDA doesn't recommend serving rare steak.

Rare [130°] Not Recommended

Medium rare [145°]

Medium [160°]

Medium well [165°]

Well done [170°]

# Essential Techniques for Grilling Seafood, Kebabs, and Vegetables

Become a grill master with these techniques for fish and shellfish, kebabs, and veggies.

## How to Grill Fish

• When you grill seafood, it's particularly important that the rack be very clean. Any residue on the rack could interfere with the seafood's delicate flavor; a clean rack also helps prevent sticking.

• Lightly spray the grill rack with cooking spray before placing it over the coals. This keeps the food from sticking and makes the grill rack easier to clean.

• You should always place seafood on a hot grill rack and leave it there for several minutes before you try to move it. This way, a sear will develop between the fish and the grill rack, which will further help to prevent sticking.

### Fish That Can Take the Heat

The most important thing to know when grilling fish is what kind to use. You want fish that has a thick, firm, meaty texture so that it won't fall apart while it's cooking. Although some firm-textured fish tend to be higher in fat than other, more delicate fish, it's the type of fat that's heart-healthy. Here are some of the fish that are well suited for the grill.

**Grouper:** This white-meat fish is sold in fillets and steaks. If you can't find grouper, you can use sea bass or mahimahi.

**Halibut:** The meat of this fish is white and mild-flavored and comes in steaks and fillets. Although it's a firm fish, it's a tad more delicate than the other fish in this list, so be gentle when turning it on the grill.

**Salmon:** With a range of flavors from rich to mild, salmon can take on a char and still keep its distinct taste. Salmon's pink meat comes in steaks and fillets.

**Swordfish:** This mild but distinctive-tasting fish has firm, gray-white flesh and a meaty texture. Its natural oil content keeps it moist while grilling. You can usually find it sold as steaks.

**Tuna:** If you're new to grilling fish, fresh tuna is a good place to start. It cooks like a beefsteak, and its deep red meat almost never sticks to the grill.

### Shellfish That Can Take the Heat

**Scallops:** This bivalve is usually classified into two groups: bay scallops and sea scallops. The larger sea scallops are best for grilling because, like shrimp, they have a meatier texture and can be easily skewered. They cook fast, though, so keep a close eye on them.

**Shrimp:** Large shrimp are best for grilling. They can be easily skewered, and they cook quickly.

### Checking for Doneness

To avoid overcooking seafood, go with a medium-hot fire rather than a really hot one. You should start checking fish several minutes before you think that it's done. There are a couple of ways to do this: There's the old standby method of testing for flakiness with a fork. Or you can also make a small slit in the thickest part of the fish with a sharp knife. Cooked fish will be firm to the touch and opaque; undercooked fish will appear shiny and semitranslucent.

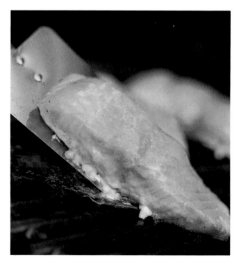

# How to Grill Kebabs

You may call them shish kebabs or skewers: They're the same thing. Kebabs are accommodating and easy to customize; they're a natural for mixing ingredients, flavors, and cooking styles. And kebabs are as easy to serve as they are to prepare.

### Skewer Savvy

Here are our tips for skewering success.

• Soak wooden skewers in water for 30 minutes so they won't burn on the grill.

• When grilling meat kebabs, be sure the pieces are all the same size to ensure even cooking. Pounding chicken to an even thickness helps it cook quickly and evenly.

• Shrimp, scallops, and other wobbly bits benefit from the double-skewer technique: Thread the pieces on a skewer, then run another one through the pieces parallel to the first, about a half-inch away.

• Cook meat and vegetables on separate skewers, so those who don't want meat can pick up a skewer of vegetables. If your family or friends assemble their own skewers, place meat and vegetables in separate bowls.

• If the weather isn't good for grilling, you can broil kebabs; it doesn't take any longer than grilling.

## How to Grill Vegetables

Grilling adds a whole new taste sensation to veggies, especially when they take on a chargrilled flavor as well as look. Depending on the recipe, you can either grill the vegetables first, then slice them, or you can slice first. If the vegetables are large enough, you can place them directly on the grill. If not, you can use a grill basket. The best vegetables for grilling are sturdy ones such as eggplant, yellow squash, zucchini, tomatoes, bell peppers, potatoes, and onions.

### Grill Baskets

Grill baskets work fine for grilling pieces of vegetables and some types of tender fish. With a basket, you don't have to worry about small pieces of vegetables falling through the grill rack. However, if you don't have one, there's no real reason to go out and buy a special piece of equipment. You can grill vegetables whole, or you can cut them into large pieces, then cut into smaller pieces after you remove them from the grill.

# Subject Index

# Recipe Index